DUE PROCESS

A Plea for Biblical Justice Among God's People

DANIEL C. JUSTER, TH.D.

WESTBOW
PRESS°
A DIVISION OF THOMAS NELSON
& ZONDERVAN

WestBow Press books may be ordered through booksellers or by contacting:

WestBow Press
A Division of Thomas Nelson & Zondervan
1663 Liberty Drive
Bloomington, IN 47403
www.westbowpress.com
1 (866) 928-1240

ISBN: 978-1-5127-2305-2 (sc)
ISBN: 978-1-5127-2304-5 (e)

Library of Congress Control Number: 2015920352

Print information available on the last page.

WestBow Press rev. date: 12/18/2015

CONTENTS

FOREWORD

Daniel is right on target in his book *Due Process*. His thesis could not be more timely – or necessary. The influence of the Church has been tragically impotent despite the growth of so-called "super churches," apparent numerical growth in general, and other quantitative statistics. In fact, if anything, the church has been more and more inculturated by its secular environment so that it is often indistinguishable from the world. In its effort to be "relevant," it has increasingly modified its standards to conform to the world it is attempting to influence.

"Holiness, without which no one will see the Lord …" is no longer sought after. Equipping the laity for ministry has been reduced to programs and methods, rather than "training in righteousness," for which purpose the Scriptures were inspired (2 Timothy 3:16).

For all practical purposes, the church has ceased to influence the contemporary culture – spiritually, morally or ethically.

Richard C. Halverson
Former Chaplain of the United States Senate

INTRODUCTION

With regards to the Body in America at the beginning of the 21st century, the words of the prophet certainly hold true: "*They do not know My ways*" (Psalm 95:10, cf. Hebrews 3:10). Today, most people who claim to be followers of Jesus do not understand God's standards of righteousness and justice. It is not that we are striving toward that standard and falling short. Rather, we do not even know what our Father expects of us. Our Christianity has taught aspects of the basic gospel using modern media, but most members of the Body are creatures of shallowness. They have not delved into the Scriptures to understand the ways of God. Popular conceptions of God's ways are at war with the teachings in the Scriptures. The Body is called to be a city on a hill, a light shining in darkness, and the salt of the earth. We are instead a laughingstock of fallen clergy and people full of slander, with children in rebellion and compromise with the dominant culture. The character of the Body in America is at a low ebb, and it shortly will be shaken to the core, revealing the foundation or lack thereof of everything in it.

Who am I to make such a statement? Have I been a rabble rouser in the Body? No, such is not my nature. My motive stems from a deep love for the many streams of the Body. At twelve years of age I accepted Jesus as Lord and Messiah. My early years of discipleship in an evangelical Reformed Church and in fundamentalist Bible Clubs introduced me to people who were sold out to the Lord. I have known many who were the salt of the earth. A righteous elder in this Reformed Church was instrumental in leading me into the experience of immersion in the Holy Spirit. At the King's College in Briarcliff Manor, New York, I met righteous professors whose love for the Lord and conformity to His character were more central than academics. I continued to find people with these character qualities at Wheaton College and at Trinity Evangelical Divinity School. Some, even in these highly academic atmospheres, sought the presence of the Lord, faithful character traits, and a walk with Him more than all other pursuits. My spiritual father at Wheaton, Chaplain Evan Welsh, was the most righteous man I have ever known. He was without peer in love, character, and saintliness. Our Lutheran pastor in Wheaton, Theodore Laesch, was a servant of great faithfulness and love. Yes, I have had disappointments in the Body, but my experiences by far have been good. It was through the influence of Chaplain Welsh that I was ordained into the Presbyterian denomination. Providentially, Dr. Welsh was the instrument of my entering into my life's work: seeking to win and nurture those of the house of Israel.

Upon entering the Presbyterian pastorate, I knew that I was entering a denomination that had drifted from its Scriptural roots. I hoped to be an influence in its return to these roots. Although not all the emphases in historical Presbyterianism are my "cup of tea," many wonderful and exemplary things can be said for historic Presbyterianism. My taking leadership in the growing Messianic Jewish congregational movement (from 1972 to the present) eventually made my leaving the Presbyterian denomination a practical necessity. These ties were sadly left behind. Additionally, my desire to identify with the rest of the Body caused me to seek fellowship with groups of leaders who pastored independent charismatic congregations.

As part of my responsibilities with the Union of Messianic Jewish Congregations, I was traveling extensively to interdenominational conferences and to congregations of all stripes throughout America. It was a great shock to discover the state of many of the congregations, both in my own city and around the country. It was especially so in the charismatic groups to which I most wanted to relate. A "sloppy agape" where almost "anything goes" had become pervasive in the Body.

Nothing that will last can be built without standards of righteousness, justice, and due process. Otherwise we will cancel out one another's efforts in competition and mistrust. It will not be long before satan attacks and sends difficulty. Along with prayer and spiritual warfare, establishing God's standards of righteousness and justice are absolutely essential if the Kingdom of God is to prevail. However, God has promised that His Kingdom will prevail. Therefore I have to believe that His standards will be established again among His people.

My understanding of the Body is a radical one. I believe that we are to be a company of committed people who were soundly converted to the Lordship of Jesus. As a result, we are to be a people who have two primary goals in mind. Our first goal is to be conformed to the character of Jesus, as well as His charisma – Holy Spirit life, faith, and gifting. Secondly, we are to love the lost, that they might come into a covenant and relationship with Jesus. Our initiatives and activities must foster these goals. Out of them issue all other righteous goals, including influencing society toward righteous standards, reflecting the glory of God in the arts, discovering more about His world in the sciences, and any other worthy goal. However, all is to flow out from a people who consider the pursuit of the first two goals as the way in which we live, move, and have our being. The character of Jesus includes the first great attribute of righteousness: to love the LORD with our all. It is to know Him and make Him known. Scriptural liberty is never the right to do as we desire, rather a change of our desires so that what we want to do is according to His holy standard. This change is a product of His life in us. This is true freedom in the Scriptural sense.

We read of the Messiah in Isaiah 42:3c-4 – *"He will bring forth justice for truth. He will not fail nor be discouraged, till He has established justice in the earth; and the coastlands shall wait for His law.*" If what these verses describe is the orientation of Jesus, it should be ours as well. If justice is to be established on the earth, His followers must be a community of love and justice.

We now turn our attention to answering this question. May the Lord use this modest book in some measure to turn His people toward the righteous pursuit of justice. May our motive of this endeavor be love!

Addendum to Introduction

Since the first publication of this book in the early 1990s, we still have not seen a shift in the Body on the issues of character standards, congregational discipline, due process, and discipleship. Dallas Willard and others have written passionately about discipleship and its foundation in obeying the commandments of Jesus. Yet discipleship is rare, and the definition of love as indulgence is increasing. Love itself is wrongly defined, along with forgiveness, leading the indulging people into sin. We still have a continuation of leaders of very large congregations and ministries falling into sin. Additionally, the sensual culture is influencing us at a very alarming level. The statistics on the Body and internet pornography are alarming to say the least! Millennials, who claim to be disciples, may support homosexual marriage and other cultural directions that are contrary to Scripture. Indeed, many seem confused about the very foundational teaching that the Scriptures are indeed the Word of the LORD and fully trustworthy as the foundation of our teaching and practice. A mighty revival includes a depth of repentance of sin, but without the Scriptures how shall we define sin? May God use this book to make some contribution toward the path of righteousness.

CHAPTER 1

Injustice Among the People of God

The following illustrations are true, and the names have been changed for obvious reasons.

Illustration #1

It was the most blessed fellowship of pastors I had ever been privileged to attend. Ten to fifteen pastors met together weekly. The meeting was simple. Together we worshiped and shared the joys, victories, struggles and disappointments of the ministry. We prayed for one another, and the Spirit moved in prophecy to heal, encourage, and motivate. Within our fellowship were Presbyterians, Messianic Jews, Methodists, independent Charismatics, Catholic Charismatics, and some from a recently formed Charismatic Association of Churches. We truly felt love for one another.

After these brothers had met for a year, a new pastor joined the group. Pastor James was leading a newly formed independent charismatic congregation. During this period, the leader of the pastors' fellowship, Bill Nelms, began to share his love for a charismatic association of congregations in the state. He expressed his need for deeper commitment of building together beyond the fellowship. He desired to be more intensively related to this organization as well as to be a minister with a relationship to a pastors' fellowship. He invited others who would be interested to investigate this association. He assured the group that he loved the pastors' fellowship and would continue in his commitment to it. The fellowship was assured that he was not seeking to make the fellowship part of this charismatic association, for he understood that others had different denominational ties and other associations. However, it was possible that a local expression of this association might root itself in the county if others followed him into this commitment.

Most of the brothers received his sharing graciously and were supportive. However, Pastor James raised his suspicions and mistrust for that association of congregations. Indeed, at a later meeting he brought another pastor friend who had not had any relationship to the weekly fellowship. This pastor, Pastor Jacobs, was extremely antagonistic to the association of congregations that the fellowship leader sought to join. Pastor Jacobs claimed to have had bad experiences with the leader of this association of congregations and with another association of congregations that related to the first. They were all into "the shepherding movement," he asserted. He also claimed to sense a hidden agenda in in the motives of Pastor Nelms, the fellowship leader.

Many accusations were made; some answers were offered. However, the agenda of the devil was fulfilled. Such mistrust was spread that the group never recovered. The weekly fellowship of pastors in the county would never be the same. Attendance dropped off; the spirit was just not the same. We were all sad. Many accusations were made, but how should they be judged? Pastor Jacobs led one of the leading charismatic congregations in the area at that time. Many believed him. However, the groups that were charged had no day in court to respond. There was no fair judiciary to hear the evidence and render a judgment or bring peace. A wounded spirit or an unhealed hurt certainly motivated Pastor Jacobs when he forcefully put forth his accusations. Yet there was no unity in standards of covenant behavior, justice, or due process among the pastors in the fellowship. It was a fatal weakness from which the group would not recover. The fellowship died when satan found and exploited our weakness.

Illustration #2

A monthly, county-wide pastors' fellowship existed. By default, I became the leader of this fellowship. Brothers found encouragement from being together. This fellowship met monthly and included a denominational mix similar to the one described previously, as well as some Assemblies of God pastors from the area. One of the congregations in the area had undergone a major leadership crisis. Pastor Wilkens of this congregation had been caught in a homosexual tryst. The two involved had not "gone all the way," according to their testimony. Pastor Wilkens professed repentance. However, during the application of discipline, he brought many accusations against the leadership of this congregation. During this time, he allegedly spread his accusations to many others in the congregation. The congregation eventually disfellowshiped Pastor Wilkens.

To handle this difficult situation, the leaders of New Hope Church submitted themselves to seven national leaders. These seven leaders confirmed the discipline of the local congregation. Coincident with Pastor Wilkens' removal from all leadership, they advised him to receive restoration in a congregation in another state from whose ranks one of the seven came. The discipline was agreed to by all.

However, after some time had elapsed, Pastor Wilkens claimed he could not sell his house. He took that as a sign from God. He also maintained that he never was given the opportunity to present his case before the counsel of seven. Indeed, he declared that the principles of due process were severely violated. Furthermore, he insisted that the real issue was the leadership structure of this congregation and its abusive authority. He claimed to be pursuing

Daniel C. Juster, Th.D.

this issue before the sexual fall. I doubt that the inability to sell his house was a sign from God. As the old real estate adage proclaims, any house will sell if the price is low enough and the basement is dry. This leader's non-compliance with the directives for restoration, and his continued spreading of accusations, caused the congregation to disfellowship him.

Pastor Wilkens then proceeded to go and see Pastor Jacobs, whose congregation was a few miles down the road. Pastor Jacobs had major disagreements and bitterness toward the other leaders of New Hope Church. After a brief period of counsel, Pastor Jacobs and other pastors declared Pastor Wilkens restored. Shortly afterwards, Pastor Wilkens started a new congregation in the same area as New Hope Church.

Soon Pastor Wilkens showed up at the monthly pastors' fellowship. The leaders of New Hope Church stood up to excuse themselves; they explained that they could not, in good conscience, sit in fellowship with a person who was disfellowshipped. The leader of the fellowship simply could not allow that to happen. I therefore asked Pastor Wilkens to leave.

After his departure, an impassioned discussion began concerning the disfellowshipping that had taken place. The questions were many. Some were concerned that local pastors did not confirm the disfellowshipping, although it affected them. Also, why were seven leaders from around the country chosen, and not seven local leaders? It later was suggested that a local council of leaders who believe in discipline should have an opportunity to confirm the decision. After all, it was argued, it was a matter that would primarily continue to affect the Body in the local area. The disfellowshipped leader was willing for such a court to be convened. However, the elders of the New Hope Church were not willing to review the case again.

Others voiced the concern that our meeting was "just a pastors' fellowship" and should have nothing to do with enforcing discipline. (This statement implies that no standards exist for those who attend pastors' fellowships.) Even the Assemblies pastors could not see

4

how it was right to ask Pastor Wilkens to leave the fellowship. The Assemblies brothers admitted that, in their own denomination, there was usually a two-year restoration period in cases of discipline for significant sexual sin, but that it did not apply to a pastors' fellowship. Others agreed with my decision; the leaders from New Hope Church argued that not only was the disfellowshipping valid, but also that a pastors' fellowship should uphold such discipline. What was the result of this debate? The destruction of pastors' fellowship number two!

Those who did not believe in enforcing standards in a pastors' fellowship in general, or at least in this case, did not want to come if the individual involved was excluded. Furthermore, they gave credibility to Pastor Jacobs of the large charismatic congregation. He declared this disfellowshipping invalid, and with others recommissioned Pastor Wilkens. Some of the others in the monthly group who wanted to enforce standards lost their heart for pastors' fellowships and decided to simply stay within their own circles. Interestingly enough, Pastor Jacobs had a difficult marriage and family life. He was later removed from his congregation for gross sexual immorality. Did his own moral weakness influence his attitude toward discipline and restoration?

Another fellowship was dead. Those few who did not lose heart and did want to uphold standards no longer were able to gather support. The charismatic congregations of the county drifted apart with little fellowship or joint cooperation. Again there was no agreement, unity in standards, or due process that the leaders could apply to settle the issues among us.

Illustration #3

As president of a national association of congregations, I was asked to resolve a situation where one congregation had split into two. During this meeting I found that Pastor Simms of Congregation

Hope of Israel was separated from his wife and was seeing his secretary. Questioning led to the discovery of a pattern of sexual sin. I found that the pastor's marriage had been very difficult all along. That was the occasion of falling.

Why did the elders not remove him from leadership? The reason was twofold. First, they claimed that he was very intimidating, manipulative, and persuasive concerning his calling and anointing – leading to the probable negative results of his removal. Secondly, he established a constitution and bylaws whereby he could not be removed. His power in the corporation was absolute. He had copied this form of government from the Praise of Israel Congregation in another city. The leaders of Praise of Israel had spread far and wide the teaching on the rightness of this form of government. (Few were willing to take a strong public stand against this teaching in our movement.)

Our only alternative was to remove him and his group from the association. (He later did divorce his wife and marry his secretary.) We received the remaining group into the association, with its new name of Messiah Fellowship, after exhorting the leaders that they should have been stronger in confrontation in spite of the bylaws.

As a result of this situation, one of the larger congregations in our association was now defunct; few of the people continued with the new group Messiah Fellowship. People were too demoralized. Eventually, Pastor Simms sold the building of Hope of Israel Congregation and put the money in the bank. He could now do ministry by living off the interest. He now had an endowed ministry!

Illustration #4

Another leading pastor and teacher, James Scott, divorced his wife and married his secretary. The congregations he led disfellowshipped him, for they claimed he did not have Scriptural grounds for divorce. Soon afterwards he came to our area and found a ministry platform with a Christian media company. Several pastors in the area protested, only to be told that radio was a broad Christian forum with no authority to enforce discipline. Pastors in the area, myself included, sought direct testimony from the congregations involved in the disfellowshipping. Was it valid? A spokesman from these congregations claimed that although the marriage was difficult, and although there were problems on both sides (perhaps the wife was the bigger problem), before the divorce occurred the wife had been willing to seek reconciliation and counsel toward a good marriage. We were told that Pastor Scott had been unwilling. In their clear and firm conviction, he did not have Scriptural grounds for divorce and remarriage.

Today James Scott is received as a major speaker throughout much of the charismatic movement. We are told, "He repented of his sin – indeed we are all sinners saved by grace. It is not ours to judge." Yet we know of no repentance in these words: "I was wrong to divorce and remarry as I did; were I to have it to do over, I would desire to not sin against my Lord in this way. I step down from ministry for restoration. My new marriage is, however, my present responsibility."

In today's charismatic movement, divorce and remarriage without Scriptural grounds as classically understood is often permitted. If one simply is willing to tough it out and maintain the ministry, and is an attractive personality or forceful orator, acceptance will follow! There need be no process of restoration. As one prominent leader told me, to my great shock, "Who are we to judge? We are to act in love. Only God can judge and know when restoration has taken place, whether it is in a day or a year. If there is fruitfulness in the ministry, obviously God has restored."

However, how do we measure fruitfulness? Is it in the size of the ministry? Is it the number of souls saved? How will our children respond? What will become of our children's values and their perseverance through conflict when they see such examples? As one young teen asked, "Dad, is divorce okay with God?" Thank God

7

she asked. Many of our impressionable youth simply will assume that it is so. Conflict in a marriage is, in itself, not grounds for divorce and remarriage.

Illustration #5

A leading media televangelist, Jacob Gardiner, fell into sexual sin. He was part of a denomination that maintained standards for repentance and restoration. He had pledged in his ordination vows that, if he sinned in this way, he would disclose it and submit to the standards of the denomination. Before his fall, Evangelist Gardiner was sharply and publicly critical of other ministries. There was no due process in the accusations he brought forth. Soon after the denomination made its decision on the process and time of restoration required for him, Jacob Gardiner left the denomination and resumed his ministry. What about his pledge to the standards of the denomination? The Christian community is told, "We are to forgive and not judge. We are all sinners saved by grace." However, is that really the meaning of not judging? Does forgiveness mean that there is no process of restoration under human leadership?

Illustration #6

Words had been passed through the charismatic grapevine that the leader of a major association of congregations, Rev. Howard Johnson, had been in long-term, repeated adultery. However, those to whom this minister looked for accountability simply slapped his wrists, told him to stop his adultery, and allowed him to continue in his ministry. Some who are part of this association spread this report. They were greatly disappointed.

How should the Body respond to this association, its leader, and those to whom he is accountable? Additionally, are the ministers in this association and others outside it justified in spreading this report? Have they followed Scriptural standards in going to the minister and to others in charge? Indeed, should they try to see that a group of leaders hears the evidence and renders a decision regarding the minister (and even his authorities)? To not do so and to repeat the charges is to spread hearsay. After all, how do we know that the report is really true?

There is widespread mistrust in the Body concerning the leaders involved and their association. Some counsel that we are to forgive. After all, "Love believes all things. Only God can judge," we are told. Yet is this really what the Scriptures teach?

Illustration #7

Recently Pastor Dan Jarvis was approached by a friend concerning Pastor Jarvis' informal relationship with prominent national leader Rev. David Spock. He was told by this friend that David Spock was untrustworthy and had been judged by his former denomination for gross immorality from which he never repented. It was said that David Spock responded to the discipline by leaving the denomination and starting his own movement. When he approached the leaders of the denomination, Pastor Jarvis found that there was no official decision concerning Rev. Spock that they were willing to disclose. They only would state that they neither supported nor opposed his ministry. Should Pastor Jarvis separate from Rev. Spock on the basis of this report? Should he doubt Pastor Spock? Is the denomination's stance correct if they really had clear evidence of gross moral sin?

During the course of the conversation, the friend also reported an incident that happened thirty years earlier and involved another leader. According to a reliable report, Evangelist Jack Bixler, who was married at the time, was caught in bed with another woman. Other prominent leaders knew of it and since that time would have nothing to do with him. Yet there was no record of evidence, discipline, repentance, or restoration of any kind. How should Pastor Jarvis respond to this report?

Illustration #8

Rev. Sam Greenwald was part of a loose association of congregations. He reported to the executives of this association that his second wife had left him. The executives of the association advised him that although it appeared from his report that his wife abandoned the marriage (they had not yet had an opportunity to talk to the wife), under the circumstances it would be best for him to step down from the ministry and to look for another leader for the congregation. The executives made it clear that they could not require him to do so under the present standards of the association, but it would be best. Soon afterwards Pastor Greenwald left this association and joined another association that was acting in great competition toward the first group. They proceeded to make Pastor Greenwald a national figure! Pastor Greenwald brought into his new association many bad reports of the leaders of his former association. His reports were fully received and spread by the leaders of his new association.

Illustration #9

A leader of an association of congregations was publicly accused of false theology and divisive behavior by leaders in another association. Despite the lack of a fair hearing of the evidence or any due process, many were affected by these reports. Others who knew these reports to be groundless continued to support the accusing leadership. These people reasoned that it was not their battle, that they were not to take up an offense, and that their continued support of the accusing leaders was a demonstration of love which could bring change. Are these correct interpretations of Scriptural norms (love, and not taking up a bad report)? What of justice? We are told, "Justice is the Lord's. He will bring it! It is not our concern."

Illustration #10

A pastoral leader in a local congregation falls into sexual sin after becoming "burned out" in ministry. Rev. John Spaith steps down from ministry under the direction of leadership friends who are called in to provide abidance. After the requisite time of restoration has passed, the fallen leader seeks to be restored. His friends, however, perceive a different eldership calling for his life. This causes a split in the congregation. The majority asks Rev. Spaith to resume his pastoral role among them. Although the discipline of restoration was obeyed, the grounds for his stepping down were not made public. It was thought best to keep the grounds private in order to protect the man and his family.

Six years later, a split ensues between this leader and others in his congregation. Elder Bill Parish, who served as an elder before the discipline took place, knew of the situation that called for the discipline. Now six years after that situation, he brings forth many accusations in a lengthy letter, mixing the old sins with new accusations. Bill Parish, the accuser, is himself in adultery and eventually disfellowshipped! Great doubt, however, has spread concerning Pastor Spaith. Did the authorities who brought discipline six years earlier handle it properly? Should discipline be private, if at all possible, in these situations?

Illustration #11

A prominent leader of a large congregation sends out a manuscript and tapes with serious accusations against another group of leaders which oversees a large community in the same city. Pastor Jack Clements claims to have approached the leaders of this community without good results. He accuses them of prophesying falsely, teaching gross false doctrine, and prophesying by familiar spirits. These accusations cause divisions among many congregations that have established relationships with the accused leaders. Although a claim was made that Matthew 18 was followed, according to the accused leaders that is not the case. Indeed, Pastor Clements never called a council of elders to hear the evidence or a joint eldership from both groups to hear the concerns.

Finally, another minister, Samuel Leslie, investigates the charges. He finds significant areas for correction, but he does not substantiate any of the charges of gross doctrinal error, gross abuse of prophecy, use of familiar spirits in prophesying, or gross misrepresentation. Pastor Clements withdraws some of his accusations after this investigation, and he even states that his grave accusations against one prophetic leader were based on false evidence! Yet the accusations still are spread throughout the Body. Pastor Clements still claims that most of his accusations remain valid. How should this situation be handled?

The Body in America

The previous examples are only a small sampling. I wish I could say that this small sampling is exceptional. It is not. It is true that there are many good and moral leaders who seek to serve the Kingdom of God with holiness and devotion. However, even within this group there is confusion concerning the issues of government and discipline. We would not find a consensus on how these situations should be handled. The Body in America is beset by several problems, today as well as back in 1992 when this book was originally published.

First of all, we have the myths of wrong theology. Among these is the major falsehood of our day which I call "sloppy agape." Under this term I put all of the teaching that says love and forgiveness require us to forego seeing justice in the Body. Few believe that the Body should be a just society in the midst of a perverse world. Justice is often perceived as a lower Old Testament standard contrary to New Testament grace. The concepts of non-judgmentalism and forgiveness have produced an "anything goes" mentality in the Body.

Secondly, we have fragmentation among members of the Body. There are many scores of denominations and associations. The number of these groups would not be if these associations were related together and respected some common standards of righteousness and justice. However, there is such mistrust between so many of these groups that discipline in one group holds no weight with the others. A plethora of groups and associations would not be bad if they were mutually supportive and cooperative on issues of basic standards and ethical behavior.

However, in North America we like our freedom. In religious circles that means the right to hang up a shingle and start ministries. This is easier than securing a Small Business Administration loan to start a new company. Many leaders see today's congregation as entrepreneurial and competitive. There is no consensus on leadership standards for experience, training, or character. Even within associations, discipline is sometimes difficult to enforce. Many in the charismatic world have left the mainline denominational world. Because the latter has largely apostatized, the charismatic groups reject all that is within the denominational world, even the historic standards of due process forged through hard experience in the earlier days of the denomination's faithfulness!

In the mainline denominational world, true belief in the Scriptures is only found in a minority. The classic standards of the denomination are rarely applied. For example, the *Book of Order* of the Presbyterian Church was a textbook in our seminary days in 1972. I was awed by the wisdom in this manual. During the class on polity, I asked the professor if she knew of any congregation that had applied its standards and process for excommunication. For me as an evangelical, the response was amazing. She noted that it was very rare to see them applied today. However, there was one case where a Sunday school teacher was disfellowshipped because he refused to stop teaching the Genesis creation accounts as literal and would not submit to the congregation's view that these were symbolic accounts which should be squared with the theory of evolution.

A comparison of the late nineteenth century evangelical congregations with the late twentieth century charismatic and evangelical congregations (despite areas of restored truth) reveals an enormous decline in America in several areas: ethical standards for those in ministry leadership, standards for congregational membership, accountability for congregational leadership, the process of discipline for members and leaders, and the general condition of holiness. We in America are seeing the lowest standards among non-Catholics since Luther railed against the abuses and immorality amongst the Catholics.

Is the role of the Christian community completely different here compared to the role of Israel? It was God's desire that it would be said of Israel, paraphrasing Deuteronomy 4:7-8 – "*What nation is there that has a God so near and a law so just as all this law,*" which God gave through Moses. God is a God of love, but God's love must be compatible with seeking justice. Because Israel fell from God's standards of morality and justice, we read that the Name of God was blasphemed among the nations. Yet it was God's intention that righteousness, holiness, and justice would characterize Israel. That was her witness to the truth. Is there not a parallel role for the Christian community? Are the promises of God of righteousness, holiness, and justice within our ranks? Are there Scriptural, ethical standards to be enforced among those who claim to be members of the Body? Are there Scriptural standards for leaders to be enforced? Is there due process for dealing with sin, disputes, and accusations? Is it required by Scripture? How do love and forgiveness square with God's injunction in the prophets that we are to seek justice? Or with the fact that God says righteousness and justice are the foundation of His throne? Is the recent editorial in a leading Christian magazine correct when it undercut congregational discipline by claiming that only God is to judge the heart? May God lead us as we deal with these and other questions in the next chapters.

CHAPTER 2

Justice and the Hebrew Scriptures

What implications do the Hebrew Scriptures have concerning the issue of justice and due process for the Body today? First of all, we assume in this chapter that the basic thrust of the Hebrew Scriptures is valid for the New Covenant age.

The Body today lives in an abysmal vacuum concerning the issues of ethics and justice. The New Testament assumes the teaching of the Hebrew Scriptures on these issues. It does not repeat much of its content, but it makes a clear statement of its relevance (2 Timothy 3:16-17). That God is a God of love, mercy, and justice is all of one fabric in the Hebrew Scriptures; hence the relevance of Walter Kaiser's book *Toward an Old Testament Ethic*. Kaiser did not mean to write only for understanding ethics in the Old Testament period, but also that the ethics of the Hebrew Scriptures should be applied today! Yet many do not teach the ethics of the Scriptures, fearing that such teaching is too restrictive for twenty first century people!

The Hebrew Scriptures present God as a God who loves justice and who expects His people to pursue it. That is our first thesis. Our second thesis is that God established Israel to reflect the superiority of life under God's rule, a life under His principles of ethics and justice. Our last thesis is that the order of life prescribed for ancient Israel in the Hebrew Scriptures was an order in which no individual, family, leader, city, or clan was to be beyond accountability. This implies a means to pursue justice under human officials. Justice is not merely something God will bring, but something that human beings are commanded to pursue.

In the Hebrew Scriptures, justice and love are not opposites. In this perspective, it is impossible to seek love without justice. To practice, permit, or allow injustice is to destroy love. An unjust society is characterized by trampling upon others, the opposite of loving our neighbors as ourselves. Following the order of justice under the laws of God produces in a society the highest fulfillment and harmony between human beings. Mercy may be offered for the truly repentant, but the unrepentant are to be brought to justice! The Hebrew Scriptures constantly enjoin the rulers to give themselves to righteousness by bringing justice! The solution to the human miscarriage of justice is not to do away with the process of judgment, but it is to bring this process under the standard of God through righteous judges!

What is justice? It is simply God's righteous order for humanity. It is life under His rule. It is not humanistic equality where differences of gifts, roles, wealth, and calling are eliminated. It is equality before the courts. There *are* mandates for economic *opportunity.* Our prayer for the coming of God's kingdom is a prayer for Him to establish his loving, righteous rule in our midst.

The Torah: God's Standard for Love, Justice, and Mercy

Before we continue by taking a brief look at the Torah (the writings of Moses), we cannot too strongly emphasize that the Scriptural concept of justice is not the same as the humanistic one. In secular humanism, justice often means equality in the sense of sameness. It is a concept that leads to socialism. Justice, for example, would mean equality of income for all people (and a huge centralized bureaucracy to enforce it). Scriptural justice allows for differences in calling, income, wealth and gifting. However, Scriptural justice also establishes rules for opportunity whereby no class can perpetually control all wealth in a way that suppresses the poor. Opportunity, for example, is provided by the redistribution of land every fifty years and the canceling of debts every seven years. Also, a person's faith, diligence, generosity, and creativity were allowed to flourish.

Justice in the Scriptures is inclusive of the following concepts. First is equality before the law of God. Those who break a law or who have a case at law against another, whether they are rich or poor, are entitled to swift and fair justice before righteous judges. Second, justice is defined by God's standards for human relations. To act justly and lovingly is not indulgence or an application of some sociological theory whereby the criminal is coddled. Rather, justice and love are defined by acting according to the His law. Love includes an attitude of compassion toward our fellow man that seeks his highest good.

The highest good and fulfillment for man is to live in *loving fellowship* with God and man. However, Scriptural love does not overlook gross sin, even if the sinner is one's own kin. Even the closest relative is to be brought to justice by his kin for the sake of love and faithfulness to God. The highest good can be fulfilled only by living in accord with the law of God, for His law is the pattern that enables fulfillment. Yielding to behavior contrary to God's law destroys love and community. Breaking the law exacts a penalty, whether by society and its judges or by God's intervention. There is also a blood sacrifice that can bring forgiveness for many offenses. All have sinned, and all must sacrifice. Gross rebellion and its manifest acts must be punished according to the penalties of the law. To not punish sin is to leave a corporate stain on the community and to bring the whole community under the judgment of God. The Scriptures speak in corporate terms, yet they still require right behavior from every individual.

For the Torah, justice is impossible for man unless all judges serve under the ultimate Lawgiver and Judge, the Creator of heaven and earth. Thus the law in Exodus 20:2 begins with the words, "*I am the LORD your God, who brought you out of the land of Egypt, out of the house of bondage."* Love, loyalty, and gratitude toward God are the chief motives for the pursuit of justice. Fear of penalty is a secondary motive. In the Ten Commandments, we read that God is merciful and just! Exodus 20:5b-6 states, *"... For I, the Lord your God, am a jealous God, visiting the iniquity of the fathers upon the children to the third and fourth generations of those who hate Me, but showing mercy to thousands, to those who love Me and keep My commandments."*

In Exodus 21-23 there are guidelines for the judges who are to be appointed in every town. We read in Exodus 21:1 – *"Now these are the judgments which you shall set before them."* There are laws concerning servants, murder, animal control, property rights, and many others. There are laws for family life and marital purity. Sexual intercourse outside of marriage gave the father of the girl the right to require the couple to make the commitment of marriage. Adultery, bestiality, and homosexuality were punished by death. Additionally, justice in our speech toward one another is a crucial standard of covenant. Its violation brought severe penalties:

> Exodus 23:1-2; 7-8 – *"You shall not circulate a false report. Do not put your hand with the wicked to be an unrighteous witness. You shall not follow a crowd to do evil; nor shall you testify in a dispute so as to turn aside after many to pervert justice.... Keep yourself far from a false matter; do not kill the innocent and righteous. For I will not justify the wicked. And you shall take no bribe, for a bribe blinds the discerning and perverts the words of the righteous."*

A bribe with money is one type; but how much justice is foregone in the Body because of stroking, offering status, and other more subtle types of bribery?

It is my desire that we concentrate on the issue of gross slander and character assassination that is so prevalent in the Body today. This problem is intensified because there often is no process to handle significant accusations. The Torah enjoins that all cases must be decided on the basis of real evidence (in the mouth of two or three witnesses). We read in Leviticus 19:16 – "*You shall not go about as a talebearer among your people; nor shall you take a stand against the life of your neighbor: I am the LORD.*" The same Torah, however, requires us to correct and rebuke a neighbor! Leviticus 19:17 states that to not do so is to hate him. Because Israel required judicial action where there was gross sin, anyone who falsely accused another of gross sin could be brought to court and suffer the judicial penalty of that sin. We read in Deuteronomy 19:18-20 (NAS):

> "*The judges shall investigate thoroughly, and if the witness is a false witness and he has accused his brother falsely, then you shall do to him just as he had intended to do to his brother. Thus you shall purge the evil from among you. The rest will hear and be afraid and will never again do such an evil thing among you.*"

Gross slander is serious business in the Hebrew Scriptures. According to Proverbs 6:17, a false witness who pours out lies commits one of the seven sins most detestable to the Lord. There must be a just means of dealing with situations of gross slander and gossip which bring discord and separate brothers.

The Torah contains laws on showing kindness to the poor, on treating the stranger with kindness, on inheritance and much more. Great emphasis is put on respect for authority. This is especially so with regard to family life. A son who curses his father or mother is to be put to death (Exodus 20:17, Leviticus 20:9). We see in Leviticus 19:3a – "*Every one of you shall revere his mother and his father.*"

In no way can this small book deal with all of the laws of God in the Torah. However, the law of God can be summarized by the principle of loving God with our all and our neighbor as ourselves. The stranger is included as one to be so loved. Therefore, the Torah enjoins equal treatment before the courts for all people; it enjoins just weights and measures in all business dealings, and fair wages so that the poor are not oppressed! The workers are to share in the profits of the enterprise.

Appointing Judges

Not all of the laws of the Torah can be enforced. Some are for personal guidance. However, many of the laws of God can be enforced. How are the laws to be enforced when specific infractions can be proved by material evidence or testimony? The answer is in Israel's judicial system. Israel established a system of checks and balances among prophets, priests, and civil rulers. All were accountable to God. At this point we will emphasize the judges. In the Torah, Deuteronomy 16:18-20 states:

> "You shall appoint judges and officers in all your gates, which the LORD your God gives you, according to your tribes, and they shall judge the people with just judgment. You shall not pervert justice; you shall not show partiality, nor take a bribe, for a bribe blinds the eyes of the wise and twists the words of the righteous. You shall follow what is altogether just, that you may live and inherit the land which the LORD your God is giving you."

The Torah repeatedly emphasizes that the courts are especially to respect the legal rights of the poor, the fatherless, and the widow (Deuteronomy 10:18). It is far too easy for the powerful to exploit or oppress them and to break the laws of God. Although judges must not show partiality to the poor if they commit crimes, the judges are to especially see that might does not make right in Israel.

The gates were the places of judgment in each village. A village would have a population ranging from a few hundred to a few thousand people. Every village had its judges. Most individuals were to deal with the concerns in the local village. For cases that were too difficult, there was an appeal structure.

> Deuteronomy 17:8-10 – *"If a matter arises which is too hard for you to judge, between degrees of guilt for bloodshed, between one judgment or another, or between one punishment or another, matters of controversy within your gates, then you shall arise and go up to the place which the Lord your God chooses. And you shall come to the priests, the Levites, and to the judge there in those days, and inquire of them; they shall pronounce upon you the sentence of judgment. You shall do according to the sentence which they pronounce upon you in that place which the Lord chooses. And you shall be careful to do according to all that they order you."*

No One is Beyond Accountability

The structure of government in ancient Israel was a decentralized structure of judge-governors over towns and tribes. There was an appeal process to the highest court in Jerusalem. In First Samuel we read of God's great concern for Israel because of her desire for a king. However, if Israel chose a king, even this king was not above the law. That is amazing in the context of the ancient Near East. In the surrounding lands the king was the law! In Israel we are told that the king was to make himself a copy of the law (Deuteronomy 17:18) and to observe all of it so that *"his heart may not be lifted above his brethren, that he may not turn aside from the commandment ...*" (Deut. 17:20). There is nothing to indicate that the removal of the king was precluded. The process for removal is not clearly stated. Perhaps the supreme court and the leading judges could bring judgment against him if he grossly violated the law. Israel often fell to such a degree that the people followed the sinful kings. *God did raise up others with the authority to depose sinful kings.* Such was the case with Jehu. The prophetic office was used to bring rebuke. Sometimes the prophetic word would lead to the king's replacement in a coup.

There was even a process to deal with a village or city in gross violation of God's law. Could that be parallel to congregations and organizations? In Deuteronomy 13:12-18 we read that the cities of Israel were to rise up and strike a rebellious and idolatrous city. Gross sin occurred in Gibeah in Judges 19. Because the Benjamites did not stand for justice in this situation, but protected Gibeah, the whole tribe was punished by the rest of Israel. Justice clearly must be applied to corporate situations of tribes, cities, and families.

The judges act in a God-appointed capacity and represent His justice. Deuteronomy 17:11-12 (NAS) teaches the importance of respecting the decisions of the judges:

> *"According to the terms of the law which they teach you, and according to the verdict which they tell you, you shall do; you shall not turn aside from the word which they declare to you, to the right or the left. The man who acts presumptuously by not listening to the priest who stands there to serve the LORD your God, nor to the judge, that man shall die; thus you shall purge the evil from Israel."*

Therefore, contempt for the judges leads to the death penalty. All individuals are to agree with the decisions of the judges so that there might be an enforcing of justice.

God's intention for Israel as a just and loving society was related to the concept of witnessing and turning the nations back to God. In Deuteronomy 10:12-13, He asks of Israel:

> *"And now, Israel, what does the Lord your God require of you, but to fear the Lord your God, to walk in all His ways, and to love Him, to serve the Lord your God with all your heart and with all your soul, and to keep the commandments of the Lord and His statutes which I command you today for your good?"*

If the Israelites walk in the ways of God, they will have long life and be protected from disease (Deuteronomy 7:15). We read that the nations will thereby gain an understanding of God's truth in Deuteronomy 4:6-8 (NAS):

> *"So keep and do them, for that is your wisdom and your understanding in the sight of the peoples who will hear all these statutes and say, 'Surely this great nation is a wise and understanding people.' For what great nation is there that has a god so near to it as is the LORD our God whenever we call on Him? Or what great nation is there that has statutes and judgments as righteous as this whole law which I am setting before you today?"*

The severe violation of God's standards brought great judgment upon the nation of Israel. Israel was not, through most of her history, the model of a just and loving society. Idolatry and injustice came together in ancient Israel.

It is well to ask some important questions. Does the teaching of the Torah have relevance for the issue of justice in the Body today? Is the Body a just society? Are leaders and people to be accountable to judges in a fair process that considers evidence and testimony when there is gross sin or a significant dispute? Should there be a means for handling divisions between congregations and organizations? And if not, why not? Are there means for handling sin, slander, and other gross sins in the Body? In the charismatic world, is there justice today? Scripture says that these things were written for our example.

Justice: The Heart Cry of the Prophets

Right beliefs, worship, and behavior were inseparable in the faith of ancient Israel. Most members of the Body are aware that the prophets spoke with great passion when rebuking Israel for turning away from God to serve false gods. Serving the wrong gods led to additional behavior contrary to the law of God. Conversely, breaking the law of God made people more disposed to serve false gods. However, justice was at least an equal concern of the prophets.

In ancient Israel, *might was not to make right.* The worship of the one true God was to give an individual the faith and motivation to act with compassion and justice. These two concepts, compassion and justice, are not at all opposed in the prophets. It should be noted therefore that the prophets of God spoke with equal passion against the violation of the principles of justice and idolatry. This heart cry is found throughout the prophets; it ought not be missed. The judges are to be fair and objective, uninfluenced by those who bribe or manipulate politically. Micah 6:8 sums up the view of the prophets in the following famous words – *"He has shown you, O man, what is good; and what does the LORD require of you but to do justly, to love mercy, and to walk humbly with your God?"* This verse comes in the form of a scathing indictment. Micah was giving a bad report! Yes, brethren, when due process is denied and all attempts at due process have been made, there is a place for a prophetic bad report! In Micah 3:2, we are told that the leaders stripped the skin from their people. Indeed, God spoke the following in Micah 6:11-12 – *"Shall I count pure those with the wicked balances, and with the bag of deceitful weights? … Her inhabitants have spoken lies.*" We also read that Israel sold the righteous for silver and the poor for a pair of sandals (Amos 2:6). The corruption of the court system was a key to sin's flourishing, yet most congregations have no court system! What are the implications? We read the following of the court system or the judges of the gates:

> Amos 5:10-15 (NIV) – "*There are those who hate the one who upholds justice in court and detest the one who tells the truth. You levy a straw tax on the poor and impose a tax on their grain. Therefore, though you have built stone mansions, you will not live in them; though you have planted lush vineyards, you will not drink their wine. For I know how many are your offenses and how great your sins. There are those who oppress the innocent and take bribes and deprive the poor of justice in the courts. Therefore the prudent keep quiet in such times, for the times are evil. Seek good, not evil, that you may live. Then the Lord God Almighty will be with you, just as you say he is. Hate evil, love good; maintain justice in the courts. Perhaps the Lord God Almighty will have mercy on the remnant of Joseph.*"

Although the people of God are laughed to scorn, God's promise was and is that His people, if they have a just and compassionate society, would see the nations take positive note and remark about the wisdom in the land. We might ask, "Could Israel influence the nations for good if she was not a just society? Can the Body salt the society at large if she is not a just society. If there is no structure of justice or no clear accountability in the Body, how can we be a just society?" The devil does send wolves in sheep's clothing. We should not limit ourselves in stopping him.

It was easy for the rich to exploit the poor with taxes and slave wages. It was easy to slander and to cause the miscarriage of justice where the court structure was corrupt. Jeremiah 7:5-7 (NAS) states:

> *"For if you truly amend your ways and your deeds, if you truly practice justice between a man and his neighbor, if you do not oppress the alien, the orphan, or the widow, and do not shed innocent blood in this place, nor walk after other gods to your own ruin, then I will let you dwell in this place, in the land that I gave to your fathers forever and ever."*

Jeremiah makes it clear that being religious through Temple service would have no effect where justice was lacking! In contrast, the rule of the Messiah is one that will bring justice in the land. Jeremiah 23:5 (NIV) states – *"The days are coming,"* declares the Lord, *"when I will raise up for David a righteous Branch, a King who will reign wisely and do what is just and right in the land."*

In the writings of the prophet Isaiah, we have the most passionate plea for God's people to be a society of justice. Isaiah constantly provides us with a contrast between Israel with her injustice, lack of standards, and unholiness with the just society that the Messiah will bring. Let us remember that we are the Body of the Messiah. We are to reflect His ways and bring His will into manifestation among His people.

The Messiah is a judge; we read of His supernatural discernment in Isaiah 11:3-4 – *"... He shall not judge by the sight of His eyes, nor decide by the hearing of His ears; but with righteousness He shall judge the poor, and decide with equity for the meek of the earth ...."* Members of the Body are often poorly taught; many do not realize that this passage is speaking of the Messiah as King-Judge in the sense that He renders just decisions where issues and conflicts arise among human beings. Is He only to do this directly, or also through His people?

The prophets greatly valued the judicial function. It was a central issue for them that people be trained in character and wisdom for judicial functioning. That is far from today's understanding. Although we bring the lost to Jesus, we fail to prepare a just, local congregation where these new members of the Body can properly mature. In contrast, Isaiah writes these words of the Messiah in Isaiah 42:3-4 – *"A bruised reed He will not break, and smoking flax He will not quench; He will bring forth justice for truth. He will not fail nor be discouraged, till He has established justice in the earth; and the coastlands shall wait for His law."* Due process and the courts of justice are meant to protect the righteous against the crimes and onslaughts of the wicked. His law is the key to the meaning of justice. Do we not have many wolves in sheep's clothing in leadership and in the ranks of the Body who slander, extort, commit adultery, and abuse the sheep? Yet where is there any means to deal with these people? Are we merely to pray until God zaps them? That will indeed eventually happen, but it is hardly merciful to them. A process of justice might bring them to their senses and to repentance. In the Hebrew Scriptures, the meaning of rulership is connected to the dispensing of justice.

Isaiah's Great Justice Chapter

Isaiah's most passionate chapter on justice, in my view, is the magnificent fifty-ninth. The opening verses show that Israel was calling upon God for national deliverance. However, their sins had separated them from God and His deliverance. God, therefore, had hidden His face from them. What were these sins? We read in Isaiah 59:3 – *"For your hands are defiled with blood, and your fingers with iniquity; your lips have spoken lies, your tongue has muttered perversity."* Then, contrary to teaching that encourages members of the Body to be silent and passive in the face of injustice (e.g., do not take up an offense for another, be loving to all sides in disputes, do not take sides, etc.), Isaiah 59:4 says – *"No one calls for justice, nor does any plead for truth. They trust in empty words and speak lies; they conceive evil and bring forth iniquity."* In other words, God's people are to stand up against injustice! Our lack of teaching on this subject may be the reason why we seem so apathetic about the great issues in our land today.

We are not to take a stand outside of Scriptural principles and processes. We are not to take up offenses in the sense of being bitter and vengeful for the sake of another. However, when the principles of justice are trampled, love demands that we stand for justice. That is the clear lesson from those who stood with the Jewish people in the Holocaust and from those who gave lame excuses not to do so. Then Isaiah describes the plotting of the wicked, the deceit on their lips, and their distance from justice. The lack of justice produces a terrible condition:

> Isaiah 59:9-13 – *"Therefore justice is far from us, nor does righteousness overtake us; we look for light, but there is darkness! For brightness, but we walk in blackness! We grope for the wall like the blind, and we grope as if we had no eyes; we stumble at noonday as at twilight; we are as dead men in desolate places. We all growl like bears, and moan sadly like doves; we look for justice, but there is none; for salvation, but it is far from us. For our transgressions are multiplied before You, and our sins testify against us; for our transgressions are with us, and as for our iniquities, we know them: in transgressing and lying against the LORD, and departing from our God, speaking oppression and revolt, conceiving and uttering from the heart words of falsehood."*

Then come these ringing words in Isaiah 59:14-15 – *"Justice is turned back, and righteousness stands afar off; for truth is fallen in the street, and equity cannot enter. So truth fails, and he who departs from evil makes himself a prey."* These are judicial words. False testimony causes truth to fall in the street. Equity cannot enter, for equity is balanced and sound judgment is based on Scriptural wisdom. In a circumstance like that, the righteous are persecuted: *"he who departs from evil makes himself a prey."*

Again God makes it clear that He expects His people and leaders to stand for justice, to stand against gross injustice and to depart from those who practice such. Isaiah 59:15-16 states – *"... Then the LORD saw it, and it displeased Him that there was no justice. He saw that there was no man, and wondered that there was no intercessor ...."* Note that verse sixteen is usually applied to intercessory prayer – that we would pray for the spirit of revival, mercy, and forgiveness for our land. That is a true, but secondary, application of the verse. If we have a heart for people, of course we want them to repent and to know God. We want to see His deliverance on this basis, not His judgment. However, our religious tradition has blinded us to the primary meaning. God was amazed that there was no one to stand in the gap and call out for justice for those who were denied it! An intercessor is one who stands alongside the one who is denied justice and cries out for it. On this basis, those who stood with the Jewish people during the Holocaust were intercessors. Sometimes an intercessor goes to death or receives persecution when standing with the oppressed. The denial of due process and justice under the law is oppression!

Therefore, what will God do? He will bring justice indeed, but His judgment will be severe! If human instruments under God do not do justice, a more severe judgment will fall upon the land. We see in Isaiah 59:16-18:

"... Therefore His own arm brought salvation for Him; and His own righteousness, it sustained Him. For He put on righteousness as a breastplate, and a helmet of salvation on His head; He put on the garments of

vengeance for clothing and was clad with zeal as a cloak. According to their deeds, accordingly He will repay, fury to His adversaries, recompense to His enemies; the coastlands He will fully repay."

It is a Scriptural principle: Unjust societies will eventually perish with severe judgment. What does this suggest for unjust congregations and movements that claim the name of Jesus?

Clearly when the means of due process and justice are denied, it is the responsibility of the members of the Body to separate from injustice and stand as an intercessor with those who are grossly and unjustly treated. I believe that doing so would greatly change the whole nature of the Body today and would be a great beginning toward holiness. The Scripture makes it clear that cases of gross sin and error are to be brought before those who sit as judges. The understanding of this principle and its application would greatly diminish the ability of evil leaders to destroy ... and of unrepentant people to find a home in the Body!

Justice in the Psalms

The Book of Psalms is filled with expressions that call for the establishment of justice. For some, the call for justice in these psalms is part of a sub-Christian Old Testament perspective. These psalms almost are cleansed of their import for these people, similar to unbelieving scholars removing the miraculous in their interpretations. It is true that the Psalmist did not have our full perspective on spiritual warfare; he did not have the name of Jesus and the power of the blood of the Lamb to defeat the forces of the enemy. Yet what of his heart to establish justice? Was it an accurate and trustworthy orientation? The Body has wrestled with the Psalms that call for vengeance upon human enemies, so several comments are in order here.

I believe it is true that most of the calls for vengeance on enemies are to be applied to the demonic hosts that war against us. As Paul aptly taught, we wrestle not against flesh and blood, but principalities and powers in the heavenlies (2 Corinthians 10:4), as satan works through some kind of invitation from man. However, it is possible by the Spirit of God to also pronounce judgment upon man. Yes, our attitude toward people in general is to be one of love and compassion, whereby we seek their redemption. However, is there potential for a person to become so wicked that, after a certain point, a proper attitude is to pray that God's judgment may fall upon them? That certainly seems to be the case with the saints in the Book of Revelation toward the antichrist and his leaders.

Secondly, I believe that the emphasis in the Psalms on the king of Israel and the Messiah bringing justice to society has significant implications for leaders in the Body now. Although this theme is pervasive in the Psalms, it is truly amazing how little attention it receives. It is almost as if only those passages that are for comfort or are predictive of the Messiah's coming have any relevance!

To be in accord with God, who hates wickedness, must certainly be proper. Although we all must remove personal vengeance from our hearts, to preach an easy forgiveness is wrong – where in our forgiving others there is no stand to call them to repent of gross sin. We read in Psalm 5:4-6, 9-10:

> *"For You are not a God who takes pleasure in wickedness, nor shall evil dwell with You. The boastful shall not stand in Your sight; You hate all workers of iniquity. You shall destroy those who speak falsehood; the LORD abhors the bloodthirsty and deceitful man. ... For there is no faithfulness in their mouth; their inward part is destruction; their throat is an open tomb; they flatter with their tongue. Pronounce them guilty, O God! Let them fall by their own counsels; cast*

them out in the multitude of their transgressions, for
they have rebelled against You."

The pleas in Psalm 7:9-11 are powerful indeed – "*Oh, let the wickedness of the wicked come to an end, but establish the just; for the righteous God tests the hearts and minds. My defense is of God, who saves the upright in heart. God is a just judge, and God is angry with the wicked every day."* The character of God and of the Messiah in administering justice is clear in Psalm 9:8 – "*He shall judge the world in righteousness, and He shall administer judgment for the peoples in uprightness."*

Another call for justice in the face of man's treachery is powerfully brought forth in Psalm 12:1-3 – "*Help, LORD, for the godly man ceases! For the faithful disappear from among the sons of men. They speak idly everyone with his neighbor; with flattering lips and a double heart they speak. May the LORD cut off all flattering lips, and the tongue that speaks proud things."* This cry for vindication for the just, and punishment for the wicked and the unrepentant, is consistently part of the fabric of the Psalms.

Psalm 37 is one of the most magnificent psalms that deal with the theme of wickedness. The justice of God is again in view in Psalm 37:27-31 – *Depart from evil, and do good; and dwell forevermore. For the Lord loves justice, and does not forsake His saints. … The mouth of the righteous speaks wisdom, and his tongue talks of justice. The law of his God is in his heart; none of his steps shall slide."* Since God is the righteous Judge, a people of righteous character will seek to establish justice in the midst of the earth. Intense desire for God to judge the wicked is pervasive in Psalms 58 and 59. God assures the writer of Psalm 76 that with the proper timing, He will fully bring judgment and justice to those who are under the burden of unjust authorities.

Psalm 82 is a stirring call for the judges or leaders in Israel to act with true justice in their courts. God is the Judge of the judges. We read in Psalm 82:1-4 – "*God stands in the congregation of the mighty; He judges among the gods* [judges]. *How long will you judge justly, and show partiality to the wicked? Selah. Defend the poor and fatherless; do justice to the afflicted and needy. Deliver the poor and needy; free them from the hand of the wicked.*" Psalm 84 contains another stirring call for God to judge the proud and rebellious. We also gain new insight into Psalm 119 if we read it as a guide not only for the individual, but also for leaders and judges among the people of God. Finally, Psalm 141 calls upon God for safety from wicked schemes. However, it indicates that the reason schemes can be effective is that there are wicked leaders or judges. When righteous and just judges reign over the people of God, wickedness cannot be established. Thus we read in Psalm 141:6a – "*Their judges are overthrown by the sides of the cliff.*"

The wisdom in Proverbs gives a full account of the differences between the wicked and the righteous in many areas of life. The law of God provides the source of wisdom for rendering fair judgment. It is amazing to see how far the Body of the Messiah has departed from these sentiments! Have we not created our own interpretive grid or approach to the Scriptures, in which this major emphasis of justice is hardly a part of our emphasis? Of course, the reader will often hear that these teachings are from the Old Testament and that the New Testament presents a different ideal. But does it? Our next chapter shall address this question.

CHAPTER 3

The Justice of God in the New Testament

The words of Jeremiah 5:1 are true for many segments of the Body in America today – "*Run to and fro through the streets of Jerusalem; see now and know; and seek in her open places if you can find a man, if there is anyone who executes judgment, who seeks the truth, and I will pardon her.*" Many in the Body do not believe that the congregation today is to be a just society, with the processes and structure to secure justice. Love has been viewed as the opposite of justice rather than as the motive to seek justice. Some think that justice is a proper concern of our society at large, and even that the Body is to seek to influence society to justice. However, that the Body itself is to be a just society is a wholly new thought for many!

The Background of New Testament Teaching

The New Testament assumes the teaching of the Hebrew Scriptures as the background for its true understanding. However, the structure for obtaining justice in New Testament days was quite different than in the days of Israel's kings. One important difference was that Israel did not have her independence, but she was kept by force within the commonwealth of the Roman Empire. The ultimate jurisdiction for many justice issues was the Roman court. That especially included cases where the penalty was capital punishment. However, Jewish courts still functioned within the land of Israel. The Romans were fully willing to allow these courts to handle many types of cases. Exactly where the jurisdiction of the Jewish courts ended and where Roman courts were mandated is a matter of some debate. It is especially debated with regard to the stoning of Stephen, the trials of Paul, and specifically in the crucifixion of Jesus.

It is plain that at the time of Jesus, the highest Jewish court of appeal was the Sanhedrin. We do not read of such a body in the Hebrew Scriptures. In the Hebrew Scriptures, the high priest had a major judicial role. The Sanhedrin was made up of leading elders from different religious parties in Judaism (Sadducees and Pharisees). The Sanhedrin, as the supreme court, could decide to hear a case or to not receive an appeal. If they decided not to hear an appeal, the decision of the lower court would hold.

What, however, were the lower courts? It would appear that in the inter-testamental period, the institution of the elders of the gate was replaced by the elders of the synagogue. Therefore, the synagogue functioned in judicial matters, especially on religious questions. More serious questions still could be heard by leading elders of a city. That the synagogue was ruled by men who were called elders clearly indicates their judicial function.

Despite all of the debate concerning which religious party Jesus was the closest to (Pharisees, Sadducees, Essenes and Zealots), it is clear to me that Jesus was closest to the viewpoint of the Pharisees. Hence, in Matthew 23, Jesus taught that the scribes and Pharisees sit in Moses' seat. People were to follow their decisions. Jesus was not teaching that His disciples had to believe in all manner of Pharisaic doctrine and religious practice. His example is clearly at variance with that idea. Rather, He recognized that their legitimate function was to serve as the judges in the courts throughout most of the land of Israel. They performed the function of judgment that was carried out by the elders of Israel whom Moses had appointed. Citizenship in Israel required following the law of the land and the decisions of the courts where such was not contrary to the Scripture. I believe that by this time, the courts of Israel were mostly in the hands of the Pharisees. However, the high court was composed of mostly Sadducees, with Pharisaic representatives. In ancient Israel, appeal went from judges who were not Levites, to the high court which was Levitical.

The New Testament Parallel

Jesus' instruction is similar to how we would instruct members of the Body today to be good citizens in whatever land they reside. It includes obeying the laws of the land and the decisions of the courts where they are not contrary to Scripture. Paul enjoins the same for the faithful under the Roman government (Romans 13). One must disobey where the law is against Scripture.

Jesus Establishes a Society

However, from Matthew 16 it becomes clear that Yeshua is forming His own society or congregation (Hebrew: *kehilah*). *Kehilah* is a term that can refer to a synagogue. This congregation, which will be made up of many congregations, is to be built upon the confession of the fact that Yeshua is Messiah and Lord. This society will be a righteous remnant in the midst of Israel and eventually in all of the nations of the world.

The announcement of the Kingdom of God in Jesus' preaching prepares us for this society. The Kingdom of God theme, as expressed in the prophets, looked forward to an ideal age in which the nations will come to the knowledge of God, and peace and prosperity will be fully manifested. Jesus' announcement brought a new stage of the Kingdom of God where the realities of the age to come broke into this age. The Kingdom came in Jesus, but it has not yet come in fullness. One key manifestation of the Kingdom of God will be that God's law and justice will be established in the earth. So in this stage of partial fulfillment of the promise of the Kingdom, in this transitional age, the manifestation of justice and righteousness is to be the society that Jesus established on the basis of Peter's confession in Matthew 16:16 – *"You are the Messiah, the Son of the living God."*

This gives us a key for understanding the relationship between the Hebrew Scriptures and the New Testament. The Hebrew Scriptures present us with a limited manifestation of the Kingdom of God. In the Hebrew Scriptures the power of the Holy Spirit was not available to all. Furthermore, the hope of the prophets, that all nations would come to the knowledge of God, was rarely demonstrated. In the New Covenant the Kingdom is extended to the nations, and Jew and Gentile come under the rule of Jesus. It is a stage of Kingdom manifestation that looks forward to the coming of the Kingdom in fullness, even the Age to Come.

The Kingdom in this transitional age is seen in the lives of believing individuals and families and the areas they touch – and especially in the life of the Body. This congregation of Yeshua does not wield the sword, and her courts do not have the power of corporal punishments or imprisonment. However, the Body is to be a just society that can require repentance, reconciliation, restitution and restoration – or ultimately disfellowshipping – as its means of maintaining itself as a just society. The chapters of Matthew 16, 18 and 21 provide us with clear teaching on the nature of this new society, the way it is to be governed, the principles of due process by which justice will be established in it, and the fact that the rule of the elders of this society is to take precedence over both the Sanhedrin and the elders in Israel who do not follow Yeshua the Messiah.

The Meaning of Binding and Loosing (Matthew 16, 18)

Matthew 16 records Peter's great confession of Jesus as the Messiah, the Son of God. This confession is the basis, or foundation, of the congregation that Jesus will build. Jesus then said in Matthew 16:18-19 (NAS) – "... *I will build My church, and the gates of Hades will not overpower it. I will give you the keys of the kingdom of heaven; and whatever you bind on earth shall have been bound in heaven, and whatever you loose on earth shall have been loosed in heaven.*" Many have taken this passage as a foundation for our authority in prayer, and rightly so. However, I do not believe that that is the primary meaning of the passage. The keys of the Kingdom had a specific meaning within Judaism at the time, as reflected in the Talmud. The keys were understood to be the delegated authority for judicial decisions in Israel, the covenant nation. The members of the Sanhedrin, as the highest court in Israel, understood themselves to possess the keys to the Kingdom of Heaven. The keys were understood to include the right to permit some activities and to forbid other activities. To bind is to forbid, and to loose is to permit. Two or three judges in the name of Jesus can make such a decision. Jesus is in the midst of such a court and backs the decisions done in His name and will. Even so, the Talmud makes it clear that three judges form a proper judicial court (Hebrew: *Bet Din*). After the fall of Jerusalem and the disbanding of the Sanhedrin, the leading rabbis understood themselves to have this authority. This situation is reflected in the Talmud as well. (The Talmud is a compendium of Jewish law, debate, story, and legend. It was put into a written format from the third to the sixth centuries.)

Chapters 16, 18 and 21 of Matthew record the incidents whereby our Lord transferred spiritual authority from the Sanhedrin to the apostles. Matters governing the behavior of the members of the Body were ultimately in the hands of the apostles. Jesus did leave realms of civil authority in the hands of both the Pharisees and the Roman authorities. However, the higher authority of the apostles included the areas of correct Scriptural doctrine and behavior. Following the dictates of either the rabbis or the Roman authorities had to be within the boundaries of gospel standards. Hence Peter's famous response to the illegitimate exercise of authority in Acts 5:29 (NAS) – *"We must obey God rather than men."* In Matthew 16, this new authority of the apostles is established through Peter as representative and head of the apostolic band.

Matthew 18 provides us with another installment in the process of transferring authority, as verse 15 begins by noting the proper procedure for dealing with a brother who has sinned. The one who is sinned against is to go to that brother and seek to restore him, thus gaining him back. If the brother who sinned will not hear, the other is to bring two or three brothers to stand as witnesses to the confrontation. Matthew 18:16, quoting Deuteronomy 17:6, states – *"By the mouth of two or three witnesses every word may be established"* which immediately places us in a context where judges render a decision. A decision of guilt should be based on the clear and solid foundation of credible witnesses. These witnesses are to urge the brother to repent. Following such a procedure shows us that the sin is serious. If the brother repents at this stage, no judicial action is necessary. We note, however, that certain kinds of sins disqualify persons from leadership positions in the Body, at least for a time. (In these cases, there is still a need to bring out the truth so that the brother will step down from leadership for restoration, even if sin is acknowledged and a profession of turning from it is made.) If there is no success at the second stage, the witnesses tell the congregation through the leadership. That gives the congregation an opportunity to plead with the brother or sister, hoping that a response of repentance would come about. However, if even the congregation cannot win him or her to repentance, then we read in Matthew 18:17 – *"... let him be to you like a heathen and a tax collector."* This pronouncement implies several thoughts. First, it would be the elders of the congregation, who sit in judgment, who have the role of making the final pronouncement. That was the case of the elders at the gate in ancient times, the elders of the synagogue, and by implication the elders of the congregation of Jesus. The twelve disciples of Jesus are viewed as having ultimate eldership over the Body. The original band of apostles is the ultimate eldership authority for all members of the Body throughout the New Testament Scriptures. Paul and the other apostles later appointed other elders who would serve as authorities in various congregations throughout the world. These leaders also would be called upon to exercise an authority according to what is written here.

The penalty enjoined in Matthew is that the person under discipline be viewed as a pagan – a heathen or a tax collector. These are people in need of redemption! If a person cannot repent of significant sin and be reconciled to brothers and sisters, we are not to accept them as members of the congregation. Only God knows the heart, but our response should follow the evidence.

I believe that the judicial procedures of those times made it clear that the elders were to bring forth the final judgment after all the steps have been taken, saying, "With regard to the gospel, John Doe is now to be considered among us as a pagan, one who is especially in need of redemption." In the epistles we are given further instruction on how to respond to such a person, that the Name of Jesus not be dishonored.

In this context, Jesus again says in Matthew 18:18-20:

> *"Assuredly, I say to you, whatever you bind on earth will be bound in heaven, and whatever you loose on earth will be loosed in heaven. Again I say to you that if two of you agree on earth concerning anything that they ask, it will be done for them by My Father in heaven. For where two or three are gathered together in My name, I am there in the midst of them."*

The decision of disfellowshipping enjoined in this passage is connected to the judicial function of binding and loosing. It is one type of binding and loosing. There are others, such as implications for prayer in the will of God, as well as in Acts 15 whereby the Gentiles were loosed from the requirement of being Jews. However, the context is in asking God to back the judicial decisions of the leadership of the congregation of Yeshua.

Disfellowshipping binds the individual from calling himself a member of the Body in the midst of God's congregation. It also binds us to not have fellowship with him as if he were a brother. That is a clear implication of his being as a heathen or tax collector. This concept is also made explicit in the epistles of Paul.

Kingdom Authority Has Been Transferred

The parable of the landowner in Matthew 21:33-46, which is found in the other synoptic Gospels as well, brings out the truth that the authority of the Kingdom of God on earth has been transferred to the apostles. It is one of the few allegories in the New Testament. This truth is also implied in Matthew 16 and 18. However, the authority transfer is explicit in this passage.

We are presented with a landowner who put his vineyard under a group of vinedresser stewards. When the landowner sought to collect the fruit of the vineyard, the vinedresser stewards beat his servants and killed one. Other servants were sent and treated the same way. Finally the son of the landowner was sent, but they even killed the son. A question is then asked: What will the owner of the vineyard do to these unfaithful stewards when he comes? The points of reference are clear. Israel, the people of God, is the vineyard of God. The religious leaders are the stewards. They have a historic heritage of mistreating and even killing the prophets of God. Finally, they seek to destroy the Son of the Owner of the vineyard. The Son of God the Father is Jesus.

The people rightly answer the question, that the owner will destroy those wicked men and give His vineyard to other vinedressers.

For our purposes, Matthew 21:43 is especially important, where Jesus said: *"Therefore I say to you, the kingdom of God will be taken from you and given to a nation bearing the fruits of it."* This verse is sometimes wrongly understood to be a prophecy of the Christian community replacing Israel. However, the vineyard is Israel and all who are grafted into the olive tree. It is not a replacement of Israel that is in view, but a replacement of the ruling elite. The word "nation" in Greek can have broad meanings, referring to a tribe or societal group as well as to a concept related more to our modern nation-states. Obviously Jesus is speaking of an authority transfer. We read in Matthew 21:45-46 – *"Now when the chief priests and Pharisees heard His parables, they perceived that He was speaking of them. But when they sought to lay hands on Him, they feared the multitudes, because they took Him for a prophet."* This transfer of authority is from the chief priests and Pharisees to the apostles. The people did not hear Jesus teaching a replacement of Israel, but of leadership. It is clearer in the version of Luke 20:16 where the words are, *"He will come and destroy those vinedressers and give the vineyard to others ...."*

The Apostles Demonstrate Their Authority to Bind and Loose

In Acts 15 we see the effect of the transfer of authority as the apostles and elders at Jerusalem exercise the authority to bind and loose. The issue here is the prerequisites for fellowship to be placed upon Gentiles. The decision in Acts 15 does not loose Jews from Jewish calling. It does, however, loose Gentiles from the requirements of Jewish calling. They are still bound with regard to not eating blood, a standard that began with Noah, which includes not eating what is strangled. They are also to abstain from meat offered to idols and from immorality, which implies all of God's basic ethical standards of right and wrong. The Jerusalem Council acts as the high court for all members of the Body in this major decision.

On the other hand, we see no Roman-type hierarchy established by the apostles. Apparently they believed that able leaders could be called together again if necessary. The present divisions in the Body today make doing that difficult. The result of the transfer of authority is also seen in the fact that ordinary decisions of discipline are vested in local elderships, with the input of apostolic leadership.

The Appointing of Elders

The original apostles appointed elders to carry on the functions of teaching the Scriptures, of ordering the congregation in spreading the gospel, and in maintaining discipline in the life of the congregation. In Acts Paul left his congregations in the hands of a plurality of elders in city after city (Acts 14:23). They were given the authority to rule, and by implication to judge, bind, and loose.

Timothy was given the authority under Paul to appoint elders. The instructions given to him are crucial in understand the role of elders and the standards for choosing them. Titus was given similar instructions in the first chapter of the letter written to him. We shall emphasize the instructions in I Timothy 3. I believe the terms "elder" and "bishop" (overseer) describe the same function. However, this book was not written to settle the question of God's type of government structure. Most of what we say can be applied to different structures of government.

Standards for Elders

I believe that 1 Timothy 3:1-13 is one of the most "rationalized away" chapters in the Scriptures. The standards of this chapter are not impossible to meet. Yet the extent to which these standards are not enforced in the Body today is a little short of amazing.

To desire to be an overseer is a good thing. It is clear, however, that the motive should be to more fully and effectively serve others so that the Kingdom may be strengthened and expanded.

An overseer must be the husband of one wife. I believe this standard probably implies that a divorce and remarriage after coming to know Jesus is not an option for one in leadership. It disqualifies one from leadership. It certainly means that anyone who has been divorced and remarried while claiming to be a member of the Body, and who was without Scriptural grounds for divorce and remarriage, cannot be an overseer in the Body. On this point alone we see an extraordinary departure from historic standards in the Body in America today. If the personality is charismatic (which we often dub as anointed!), the backslidden leader needs only to bide his time until being accepted again as a leader by a large segment of the Body. Many will say, "Who are we to judge?" That makes a mockery of the standards apostolically enjoined.

Beyond marriage expectations, we read a list of other character traits required for one to be recognized as an elder in 1 Timothy 3:2-7:

> "... *temperate, sober-minded, of good behavior, hospitable, able to teach, not given to wine, not violent, not greedy for money, but gentle, not quarrelsome, not covetous ... not a novice, lest being puffed up with pride he fall into the same condemnation as the devil. Moreover he must have a good testimony among those who are outside, lest he fall into reproach and the snare of the devil.*"

The other standards are also extremely important, as we read in 1 Timothy 3:4-5 – "*one who rules his own house well, having his children in submission with all reverence (for if a man does not know how to rule his own house, how will he take care of the church of God)."* This verse clearly shows that successful family headship is the key prerequisite for eldership. Elder rule is given to men who have proven their ability in family life. There may be exceptions to the rule, but that is the rule! In addition, I believe that gift ministers of Ephesians 4 (apostles, prophets, evangelists, pastors and teachers) are called to fulfill eldership, or at least deacon standards.

Family headship is the proving ground because of what must be proven. In the family, a man proves his ability to discipline, to give delegated authority to his wife, and to act as judicial authority in the home. If he does these things well, he will have a well-ruled family. His judicial function will be put to the test intensely in handling disputes among his children. Children look to the parents and ultimately to the father for fair judgment in times of strife. The parents must teach the principles of love, repentance, forgiveness, and restitution through family experiences. The family thus becomes a peaceable kingdom.

Successful and Scriptural rulership in the family, with the rest of the prerequisites fulfilled, is the full and adequate preparation for recognizing eldership. If members of the Body would demand that elders have a good marriage and a rightly ordered family life, the quality of righteousness in the Body would improve greatly.

Eldership and Judicial Functioning

The designations of "elder" and "overseer" assume the judicial functions of the leaders of the congregations since the background of their use is the synagogue and its rulers. To the elders is given the responsibility of ensuring that discipling take place in a context where the gospel is being spread. True conversions provide a people willing to be discipled! In this context, the elders are to enforce the basic standards of the Scriptures for membership and the more rigorous standards for leaders.

In order to enforce these standards, the elders must be able to see that the standards of due process in Matthew 18 are followed. In addition, no leader is to ever be part of a structure of government where he is not truly accountable and thus subject to Scriptural discipline. What could be more apparent than the fact that when a leader sins in a way where he no longer fulfills the standards of I Timothy 3, he needs to step down or be removed? Today's practice is far from these standards! In an "anything goes" manner, many establish themselves as leaders simply by hanging up a shingle. There is no endorsement from other leaders or testimony that these people fulfill Scriptural standards! New Testament leaders were not self-appointed. Many today set up structures where they cannot be removed if they fall into sin! Under a misapplication of the word "forgiveness," we allow many people to continue in leadership ministries who do not fulfill Scriptural standards! How can we influence society toward righteousness when such righteousness is seriously lacking in the Body?

The Commandment to Establish Courts

First Corinthians 5 and 6 are very important chapters in clarifying the judicial function of elders. In these chapters we are given an example of how to apply standards of righteousness in a situation of gross sin. We also are provided with a list of capital offenses that require disfellowshipping, as well as a description of what that entails. In addition, there is an injunction to establish a court to settle disputes between members of the Body. If there is true repentance, 2 Corinthians makes it clear that the erring brother is to be fully received back.

In 1 Corinthians 5:1-9 we are told of a man in the fellowship who was in an incestuous relationship with his father's wife (probably a stepmother). That relationship is clearly forbidden in Leviticus 18. This issue, by the way, shows Paul's affirmation of the moral standards of the Torah for all his congregations. Paul, as an apostle, notes his judicial authority in this case in verse five. The congregation is to gather together in the power of the name of Jesus to officially disfellowship this person and to "*... deliver such a one to satan for the destruction of the flesh, that his spirit may be saved in the day of the Lord Jesus.*" Paul's instruction is in line with Matthew 18, where Jesus puts the one who sinned in the midst of his judges when the decision of disfellowshipping is made. Furthermore, the decision to disfellowship binds all congregants from fellowshipping with the person who professes to be a member of the Body but who lives in gross sin. The purpose of this severe discipline is to shock the person into sensibility and repentance. It also protects the flock against falsely professing people or wolves. There is protection in the covering of the Body. The devil might then seek to destroy the flesh with sickness. Yet even that could lead to repentance instead of to both spiritual and physical destruction.

If a person calls himself a member of the Body but continues in gross sin, he undercuts the honor of the name of Jesus. Every disciple is an ambassador in His name. The name of God is holy; all who name His name as members of the Body are to reflect that holiness. If the prophet proclaimed that God's name was profaned among the Gentiles because of Israel, how much more does the rebuke apply to the Gentiles!

The specific instructions given here by Paul lead to general instructions concerning the nature of discipline. We are told that the Body is to purge out the old leaven, a symbol of corruption and evil. The leaven of malice and wickedness must not be allowed to remain in the fellowship of the saints. Evil reports and slander destroy trust and the unity of community.

That does not mean we are not to have any contact with the lost. How then would the gospel be spread? The issue is the honor of the name of Jesus and the purity of the fellowship of the saints. Discipline is enjoined in situations of gross deception, where a person claims to be a member of the Body while living in gross sin. *It is a clear principle of the gospel. It is totally unnecessary for any truly born again member of the Body to live in gross sin. No excuse for immaturity or process of growth is allotted where gross sin is concerned. Any true conversion is an immediate turning from gross sin.* Paul makes this principle explicit:

> 1 Corinthians 5:9-13 – *"I wrote to you in my epistle not to keep company with sexually immoral people. Yet I certainly did not mean with the sexually immoral people of this world, or with the covetous, or extortioners, or idolaters, since then you would need to go out of the world. But now I have written to you not to keep company with anyone named a brother, who is sexually immoral, or covetous, or an idolater, or a reviler, or a drunkard, or an extortioner – not even to eat with such a person. For what have I to do with judging those also who are outside? Do you not judge those who are inside? But those who are outside God judges. Therefore, 'put away from yourselves the evil person.'"*

The last verse is a quote from Deuteronomy 13. God requires a basic purity to be maintained in His covenant community. Paul's teaching here is foundational. Against all of the "sloppy agape" today which says we are not to judge (a misunderstanding of the command in Matthew not to have a condemning attitude), Paul commands us to judge those inside. We can relate to all kinds of sinners in outreach. However, only those whose lives manifest basic, Scriptural moral standards may be accepted as members of the fellowship of the saints.

Disfellowshipping is the ultimate judicial sanction in the Body. The Body is not to be a civil government exacting a death penalty. However, the list of gross sins that require disfellowshipping parallel the sins in the Torah that required death or exile from Israel. That we are not to eat with such a person reflects the fact that eating together in the Jewish world has the connotation of brotherly acceptance.

A humanistic mercy often leads members of the Body to reject the claims of discipline, to the great injury of not only the person under discipline but also the Body at large. When standards of discipline are followed, the maximum potential for repentance and salvation is released. *It is a clear standard of the New Testament: that which required capital punishment in the Hebrew Scriptures requires disfellowshipping in the New Testament.*

Gross doctrinal error is presented as another ground for disfellowshipping. It is clear from Deuteronomy 13 where the people are warned against the false prophet who would call them to follow other gods. It is also plain in Galatians 1, which concerns any person who would preach another gospel. Such a person is to be placed under a curse, or by obvious implication disfellowshipped.

Do We Follow These Instructions?

We must ask several questions from this passage. First, does the Body today follow these instructions? The answer in many quarters is definitely not! Are Christians trained to maintain legitimately enjoined discipline and to avoid those who are disfellowshipped?

One of the strange facts of our contemporary congregational life is that persons in gross sin and doctrinal error are not disciplined. Leaders who become disqualified, according to standards in 1 Timothy 3, are not removed. Yet those who are not in gross doctrinal and moral error, according to Scriptural standards, are slandered and shunned for holding to differing doctrinal interpretations on nonessential matters. Many are terribly slandered and shunned without the due process of Matthew 18.

Some leaders are soft on extreme sin and error while other leaders are harsh and critical where there is no serious sin and error at all. Many times the person who is accused does not even believe the view of which he is accused. Perhaps he used a phrase or a Scriptural term that was associated with a false interpretation in the mind of the critic. Without any due process, the person is blasted from the housetops with slanderous accusations. It is the accuser who is in gross sin; for slander and character assassination is a sin that is to be punished by disfellowshipping! May God help us. Unfortunately, sometimes an adulterer is received while he calls upon members of the Body to separate from others on the grounds that their views on the timing of the rapture and the Great Tribulation are wrong! Such a scenario is not hypothetical; it has really happened. Amazingly, many follow his call!

Another fact of contemporary congregational life concerns those who seek to follow these Scriptures. It is obvious that if one congregation legitimately disciplines, with due process, its decision should be upheld and followed by other congregations. However, there is competition in the land of the free. Many leaders want more bodies in their congregations, even if growth is through lateral transfer and not from evangelism. Hence the one under discipline usually can find a congregation where the leader will receive his slanders and lies against the congregation that disciplined him. Will this leader seek to talk to the leaders of the other congregations and get the facts? Perhaps he holds to a different theology of the last days. Besides, any group that disciplines must be in the "shepherding error." At least, that is the assumption of the First Church of Anarchy. And yet, the pastor of the First Church of Anarchy will be the first to blast the group that believes in discipline as holding to false doctrine. No due process is deemed necessary before such slander is spread.

If we do not seek to uphold the decisions of congregational elders as the judiciary of the courts of the Body – to uphold discipline in an inter-congregational way – then all of the instructions of Jesus and Paul in this area are of no effect.

It is a principle of human behavior that when we do not enforce Scriptural moral standards, we fall into furthering our own legalistic standards! (The issue of inter-congregational relations with regard to upholding discipline will be dealt with in Chapter 5. The reader already has some sense of my convictions from what has been said here.) The reformers stated that God's ideal was a Body that would require unity in essentials, liberty in nonessentials, and in all things a motive of love. We have hardly followed this wonderful Scriptural ideal. What I am laying out may seem new to some; however, it is the historic position of evangelical Protestantism!

Courts to Settle Disputes

In 1 Corinthians 6, we see Paul amazed that members of the Body were going before pagans in the Roman courts to settle their disputes. Yet the saints will be the judiciary in the world to come. It is time for us to prepare by picking from our midst those who are most qualified to judge and mediate disputes. If we will judge angels, should we not even appoint those who are least esteemed among us to judge disputes, rather than to go to the courts of the world? For members of the Body to fight in the courts of the world discredits the gospel and shows that we are not a community of redeemed and reconciled human beings. It is the opposite of Kingdom manifestation. Elders are given the function to judge cases that arise. Paul says with great irony in 1 Corinthians 6:5 – "... *Is it so, that there is not a wise man among you, not even one, who will be able to judge between his brethren!*" It is better to be defrauded than to discredit the gospel. Surely, however, if we have true Scriptural elders, they could sit in judgment and weigh the evidence with the wisdom of the Holy Spirit. In making judgment, we are to keep in mind 1 Corinthians 6:9-10 – "... *the unrighteous will not inherit the kingdom of God. Do not be deceived. Neither fornicators, nor idolaters, nor adulterers, nor homosexuals, nor sodomites, nor thieves, nor covetous, nor drunkards, nor revilers, nor extortioners will inherit the Kingdom of God.*" My primary reason for dealing with these verses is to present the Scriptural truth that we are to establish courts in the Body to discipline gross sin and doctrinal error, as well as to settle disputes between members of the Body. The eldership courts also remove leaders who become disqualified and who do not voluntarily step down.

New members of the Body are like children in spiritual maturity. Thus there will always be a need for this function, to settle disputes. The verse in First Corinthians does not indicate that a member of the Body should not go to court against a pagan. He may need to do so to protect society from a criminal. But his motive should not be revenge. A disfellowshipped person could be taken to court as a pagan in some cases. However, our concern for furthering the Kingdom must always take precedence over any concern for personal justice.

The Body in the first century took these passages seriously. By the end of the century, the courts of the Body were known for their standards of fairness and justice. Voluntarily, pagans sought to submit their disputes to the courts of the Body rather than to the corrupt Roman courts.

The Body in the 21st Century

If we look at the Body in the nineteenth century, we see periodic revivals in a structure that sought to maintain basic standards with Scripturally derived principles of due process through a form of congregational courts. It was true of the Puritan movements of the seventeenth and eighteenth centuries. It was true of Methodists, Baptists, Presbyterians, Free Church denominations, Holiness denominations, and the early Pentecostal denominations that arose in the twentieth century. That does not mean they were perfect in this area. There were times when they fell short. However, there was a general consensus on those issues of discipline.

What has happened? Where are the congregational courts in the twenty first century? In our apostasized denominations, the courts exist mostly on paper. Because many historic denominations gave up their doctrinal and moral standards between 1900 and 1960, few standards are left to enforce. Other denominations no longer enforce standards like they used to (there are exceptions). Many new Christian movements believe that enforcing standards compromises freedom in the Spirit. The very concept of congregational courts would seem restrictive and deadening to the leaders of the First Charismatic Church of Anarchy. Thank God for those denominations and movements that are exceptions to this attitude.

We live in a world where anyone can appoint himself a leader. They rationalize that it is God who appoints; not man. It is true that God appoints. However it is also important that mature leaders, who fulfill the standards of 1 Timothy 3, endorse the new leaders as also fulfilling such standards. It is important that every leader be truly accountable and removable by others, according to clearly publicized processes. A planter of a new work should be *officially* accountable to outside elders. How else can the standards of these chapters and the call for enforcing such standards take place? Yes, God Himself will judge. However, to leave judgment only to Him and to not enforce standards according to Scriptural injunctions is to invite a more severe judgment. That is not mercy, but deception. We know that the apostolic leaders gave letters to accredit those who traveled in ministry, as seen in 2 Corinthians 3:1 (NAS) – *"Are we beginning to commend ourselves again? Or do we need, as some, letters of commendation to you or from you?"* In 1 Thessalonians 5:12 the Scriptures enjoin us to *"recognize those who labor among you."* To *recognize those who labor* means that we have at least ascertained their fulfilling of Scriptural standards for leadership and that they are truly accountable. Such accountability clearly was present in the Body at the end of the first century. Real accountability means submission to those who can remove disqualified leaders and who can discipline gross sin and error.

Who Should We Accept in Leadership?

Miracles alone do not attest to the identity of a servant of God. The faith of those who were ministered to can be the reason for the miracle. There are character standards for members and leaders! Because we do not act according to these Scriptural standards today, satan has many plants in the midst of the Body.

The education of members of the Body on these principles is a pressing necessity. This need is shown when a group disciplines and removes a leader, while their fans among the Christian public and other movements quickly endorse that fallen leader and make him part of themselves. In Micah 1:10, the prophet Micah proclaims – *"Tell it not in Gath."* The name of God is blasphemed among the nations, as was said of ancient Israel, because of us. May God grant us repentance that we might fully seek to follow Scripture.

CHAPTER 4

Justice and Mercy

As we begin to examine the theme of justice and mercy, it may help to start with the story in Luke 18:1-8 (NIV):

> *"Then Jesus told his disciples a parable to show them that they should always pray and not give up. He said: "In a certain town there was a judge who neither feared God nor cared what people thought. And there was a widow in that town who kept coming to him with the plea, 'Grant me justice against my adversary.' "For some time he refused. But finally he said to himself, 'Even though I don't fear God or care what people think, yet because this widow keeps bothering me, I will see that she gets justice, so that she won't eventually come and attack me!'" And the Lord said, "Listen to what the unjust judge says. And will not God bring about justice for his chosen ones, who cry out to him day and night? Will he keep putting them off? I tell you, he will see that they get justice, and quickly. However, when the Son of Man comes, will he find faith on the earth?"*

This remarkable parable makes it clear that God is very concerned for justice. Of course God is not like the unjust judge. He is the

Judge of all the earth who will always do right. In His mercy, He delays His justice that people might repent, but His judgment will come eventually. God also will avenge the persecutors of His elect, unless these persecutors repent. The martyrs in Revelation 6:10 cry out and ask how long it will be until their blood is avenged.

Sadly, many members of the Body have been indoctrinated into a gospel of indulgence in which concepts such as love, mercy, and grace are seen as contrary to justice. Many people have been taught that hellfire is for the lost, but that we who are under the blood of the Lamb have a God completely indulgent toward us so we also must be indulgent to others. To enforce historic standards for members and leaders is seen as overly organizational, unmerciful, unloving, ungracious, and even "Old Testament-ish"! Yet as the parable notes, God has not been converted from a vengeful to a merciful God since the days of the Old Testament. God has always been a God of justice, mercy, and love!

Relating Love, Justice, and Mercy

Because God loves us and is still just, we have a dilemma. How can God be accounted just by His own standards and yet forgive and bless? The answer is in the cross. The full penalty of justice was paid on the cross, and because we are in Him, we are accounted as having paid the price justice demands. To be accounted righteous, we must, by His power, repent of our sins. True repentance always includes restitution wherever it is possible. We do not deserve this grace, yet in mercy God offers it. He can offer it only because the cross satisfies His standards of justice.

The previous paragraph is a summary of the way of salvation through Jesus, as found in Romans chapters 5 and 6. A truly born again person desires to live righteously and is empowered by the Holy Spirit to turn from gross sin. After turning from such sin there is a lifetime of growth into perfection. Leaders are not perfect, but they have achieved a level of success in sanctification and fruit-bearing that causes others to look to them for discipling.

When a member of the Body sins by lying, stealing, slandering or teaching false doctrine, that person must repent. If repentance is true, the one who stole returns the stolen goods, plus extra compensation, according to Scriptural standards. Because of the cross, and of our sincere repentance and restitution, God does not hold us eternally accountable for our violation. Our sin is under the blood. However, it is not under the blood if there is no repentance. There is no real repentance if there is no restitution! The slanderer must do all in his power to restore the reputation of the individual or of the group slandered. The one who taught false doctrine seeks to inform all who were mistaught of what was false so that any wrong influence is nullified.

This process demonstrates how mercy, love, and justice come together in the plan of God. The prophets understood it. If God indulged those who "ripped off" the poor, it would not be merciful, but grossly unloving toward the victims! In Luke 19:1-10 (NIV) when Zacchaeus repented, he said, *"Look, Lord! Here and now I give half of my possessions to the poor, and if I have cheated anybody out of anything, I will pay back four times the amount."* Jesus responded, *"Today salvation has come to this house, because this man, too, is a son of Abraham."* What if Zacchaeus had said, "Look, Lord, I thank you that you are loving and forgiving; and even though I have stolen and been bad, I now receive your love"? I am certain that Jesus would not have responded positively. However, in today's world one group could require someone to repent and make restitution while another group could respond that such requirement was harsh and judgmental, that the situation was under the blood. Only sincere repentance puts sin under the blood, and there is no sincere repentance without truly desiring to make restitution.

Yes, God longs for us to receive His mercy, but He cannot provide it in such a way as to violate His justice. He longs to apply the cleansing blood of Jesus, but He can apply it only to the truly repentant. That is the nature of God's mercy, love, and justice. It is a love so deep that He sent Jesus to die for us. It is a justice so true that it required the death of Jesus for our sins and our repentance to receive it. Thus God is "just and the Justifier" of those who are in Jesus. *Those who understand God's mercy and love to be indulgence toward those who are in sin cause unrighteousness to prevail in the Body and demean the work of the cross. They have a humanistic concept of mercy, not a Scriptural one!*

One of the great problems is a lack of a Scriptural definition of justice. After decades of reflection, I do believe I have the mind of God on this. A Scriptural definition of love is fully compatible with justice. *Love is the passionate identification with the other, that perceives their worth and that seeks their good, guided by law.* Let's unpack this definition. We say love is passionate. There is an emotional component that should be under the control of the Spirit. Love is not distant from the one loved. We love because we perceive the worth of the other as in the image of God. God gives us His heart of love for the other. Secondly, it seeks their good. Good is defined in term of their destiny fulfillment on every level of existence. We are told in the Scriptures that it is God's intended destiny for every person to have a loving relationship with God and to be part of a loving community in Yeshua. Destiny fulfillment includes the areas of marriage, family, material provision, and vocation. Love is guided by law in that it is not their destiny to live contrary to the standards of God. It may seem like fulfillment in the short term, but acting contrary to God's law leads to destruction. This is why Lewis said that love seeks the perfection of the beloved, not by a critical spirit, but loving encouragement. This is how God loves us. We see from this definition that love and justice are one.

When a person truly repents and seeks to make restitution, the offended party may not only forgive so as to restore the relationship, but also forgive the debt for which restitution is to be made. That is a free gift. However, he is not free to forgive the debt for another or to release from restitution if doing so would demean the righteousness of God. At times it is more loving to require restitution, so that moral fiber might be built in the offender. With regard to monetary compensation, each circumstance should be considered. A person who habitually steals may need the discipline of restitution to grow. In cases of gross slander, the fabric of community is torn. To restore trust and love in a community, restitution is almost always necessary. So the offended party should not be required to forego restitution; such a debt cancellation is a free gift.

It is the responsibility of the elders in a local congregation, and of leading figures beyond the local scene in inter-congregational matters, to see that gross sin and error is dealt with and that restitution is made. Scriptural standards of due process and evidence must be followed. *Due process is interwoven into the whole context of the Scriptures and is a central part of Scriptural justice.*

When a Leader Falls Into Gross Sin

If a leader falls into gross sin or error, I believe Scriptural standards require that that leader be removed from leadership and undergo a process of restoration and counseling. Restoration includes public confession and requalifying. To not do so is to lower the standards of the Body. Some sins may possibly disqualify a person from leadership for life. To simply say, "I repent. It's under the blood, and God has forgiven. I am continuing in leadership," makes a mockery of Scriptural standards. Yes, God forgives. However, a truly repentant person is concerned more for the glory of the name of God. He gladly receives discipline so that God's name might be honored. The truly repentant will not see their gifts and calling as more important to God than the issue of upholding His standard of holiness and thereby glorifying His name.

Some have even lamely claimed that their continuing in ministry would help others understand that we serve a forgiving God and that we are sinners saved by grace. We *were* sinners, but we now have the power (the grace) to do right. We have no excuse for falling into gross sin. Indeed, God forgives. That the leader might be restored after requalifying is due to His mercy. God also wants to be merciful to the sheep. He knows that leaders who are allowed to remain in leadership after falling into sin and error will raise the temptation level for the sheep. "If that leader can do it and get off so easily, and is still in leadership, it may not be so bad for me to do it. I am only a lay person!"

We must recall that *forgiveness and restoration to leadership are two different things. One is the restoration of fellowship with God. The other still requires fulfilling the standards in 1 Timothy 3 all over again!*

American moral standards are at an all-time low. The Body is the salt and light that should influence society to righteousness. We surely cannot do that as long as we understand mercy and love as indulgence and the abandonment of Scriptural standards. The standards of the Body in America regarding slander, gossip, lack of due process, adultery, greed, and weird doctrines is astonishing. We recall the phrase: The world is in the church, and the church has become "of the world."

Have we not learned that allowing sin in our midst can bring a judgment on the corporate Body? Israel was defeated at Ai because of the sin of one man. To be forgiven does not mean that we continue in leadership. It means that we can experience the love and presence of God again. It means that we will not be condemned to hell. It does not mean that God's standards for leaders in 1 Timothy are to be compromised. It is dangerous to violate the standards of God; it is more so in the New Covenant because we have more power to do His will. If we do not abide by God's standards and enforce congregational discipline, God will see that justice is done eventually. By then it will be much more severe and terrifying. Is that merciful on our part?

Our Youth Need Moral Examples

We also ask for mercy and love for all of the young people and new members of the Body who need to be discipled. The example of leaders is a primary discipling force. The purpose of God's law is to direct us into the paths where real fulfillment is found. The ways which seem right to man often lead to destruction, as the writer of Proverbs noted. If we are truly merciful, we will seek to enforce standards. Then the sheep being tested will have the strongest possible example to motivate them to take the right path and find the fulfillment of God. To do otherwise is to be like the indulgent parent who will not discipline a child. True love overcomes the pain we feel in enforcing discipline for the good of the child. It is no different in the Body.

The motive for seeking justice must be love and compassion, never revenge. Justice must be sought as a high, Scriptural priority. We must check our hearts to be sure of our motives. Then we must seek to follow the injunctions of the Scriptures.

Hindrances to Love and Justice

Many people have a basic desire and an intuitive sense that there should be justice in the Body. However, the fulfillment of this desire is thwarted by false teaching and is discouraged by sin patterns among members of the Body. That is in direct opposition to the meaning of Scriptural justice. We now look to expose these issues.

The Ends Justify the Means

It is generally accepted that we believe in moral absolutes and not in situation ethics. Situation ethics is an historical position in ethical philosophy. This position was popularized by Joseph

Fletcher in his book *Situation Ethics*. Many members of the Body have not been trained in Scriptural ethics, an essential part of character development. They do not realize to what extent they act in harmony with an "ends justify the means" philosophy. For example, if they support ministers and organizations that have no solid accountability, arguing that they cannot pass up the good opportunities that follow from such an involvement (fellowship, sales of books and tapes, good preachers, etc.), then they are situationists. If they compromise with unethical leaders and groups for the sake of a false unity or of furthering some vision dear to them, they follow an "ends justify the means" philosophy.

In the classic Frank Capra movie, *Mr. Smith Goes to Washington*, the leading character battles against corruption in government. His former mentor, a leading senator, argues that his compromise with corruption was necessary to do many good things. So it is with many today; the opportunity to extend their ministries causes them to compromise with those who slander, who are doctrinally off base, who lie, who have no real accountability, or who are morally unqualified for leadership according to Scripture. Perhaps the event looks too important to pass up. Many important leaders will be there! Perhaps it is an opportunity for television. So the unsuspecting person increases the influence of unethical people.

"Ends justify the means" thinking is really a denial of God. Only true followers of God can hold to ethical absolutism – that ethical principles, understood rightly, are not to be violated and that cooperation with people who claim to be members of the Body and yet grossly break ethical principles is wrong. God is the One who gives real, lasting fruit. We are never to calculate ends in such a way that illegitimate means become a possibility. There are innumerable factors we cannot see. We do not know what God will do in bringing opportunities to those who are true and loyal. What looks like a reasonable compromise for good ends might be just what cuts us off from greater blessing.

"There is a God in Israel." What does that mean? It means we can follow the principles of the Scriptures even when it seems in the natural that the ends to be achieved will not be as beneficial. We do not have to lie, steal, or compromise with evil for a good purpose. God will see to it that in the long run, real fruitfulness will be greater. We cannot always "see it in the natural," but we live in a supernatural world where God is ultimately in control.

Suppose "Reverend Smith" goes on TV with a shady television evangelist to publicize his book. He sees the importance of getting his word out. However, he has thereby given the impression of endorsing the shady televangelist. Others will conclude, "So-and-so televangelist could not be really doing so much wrong if Reverend Smith is on the show." Perhaps if Reverend Smith had stayed true to Scripture and departed from unethical people, God would have given him his own program.

It is always dangerous to calculate the benefits that can result from compromise. Such compromise is, in part, a denial of the existence of God, or at least His control of the affairs of men. This problem is rampant today. The standards of Madison Avenue and its methods have permeated the Body. It is crucial that we depart from situation ethics. *The ends never justify immoral means.* Justification in such cases is usually un-Scriptural rationalization.

Slander

Slander may be the most insidious sin that thwarts justice in the Body today. In its worst form, gross slander spreads untrue, evil accusations against other members of the Body. Marxists trained in disinformation learned that the truth of a matter was not important in discrediting an opponent. Instead, they found that if an accusation is repeated frequently and widely, it will eventually be believed by many. Slander and gossip is so pervasive among leaders and lay people that it is beyond belief. It may be one of the greatest hindrances to revival. Slander destroys trust and tears apart the community of faith. Jesus prayed that we might be one in John 17:21. He died to create a people of love and unity. In ancient Israel, the slanderer was required to receive the penalty for that of which he had accused another. Slander could lead to death. Slander is one of the seven things hated by God in Proverbs 6:19. It sows discord, according to that writer. It is a gross sin. Yet we sometimes get away with gross slander, which is spiritual murder of their reputation!

Slander has its origin in pride, competitiveness, power-seeking, and insecurity. Strangely, these are all related traits. Discipline for gross slander should be severe, but we are indulgent. However, God included the bearing of false witness as one of the major *thou shalt not's* of the Ten Commandments. Sadly, the person who engages in disinformation in order to discredit another, a greatly prevalent practice among leaders, often comes into deception and believes the lies in spite of the evidence. He may claim to discern it in the Spirit! It should be clearly noted that *the person who hears slander and gossip without strongly rebuking the slanderer and without initiating a process of correction is an accomplice to the crime and is thus guilty!*

What if the bad report is true, or partially true? Should we be silent when there is sin? Some would teach that we should look the other way and be silent. That too is wrong. Great sin and error among us should be corrected. Yet that can be done only if there is due process. True accusations must be handled according to Scriptural standards of due process, not by private but accurate gossip! Gossip includes both false and accurate information shared outside the Scriptural order of due process.

Lack of Due Process

Without due process, the principles of justice are essentially compromised. The Scriptures provide the standards of due process for dealing with gross sin and error. Matthew18:15 shows how it is done. It has been fully explained. When sin disqualifies a leader, the situation must be brought to the attention of those who can remove the person. In some cases, even when there is repentance, the matter will need to be made public.

Due process always requires that the accused have a fair day in court before the elders. There must be two or three credible witnesses. There must be a fair judiciary that believes in the principles of repentance and restitution. Furthermore, it is crucial that the accused have an opportunity to answer his accusers before the court and to bring witnesses for his defense. To deny the accused a fair defense before impartial judges is a travesty. Many congregations who seek to discipline try to avoid the painful process of allowing the accused his defense. The witnesses for the defense must be witnesses to the issues at hand; their testimony must be useful to the case. Judges must fairly decide their relevance. It is not a time to make irrelevant, non-applicable, and non-substantiated charges against the accusers. Some who do not understand these judicial standards fear a fair defense and protect their leadership by not allowing one. That is wrong.

If the accuser refuses to deal with his accusations in a due process manner, the accuser should be disciplined for serious sin. If the accused refuses to deal with the accusations in a fair court, but responds by making counter-accusations and slandering to discredit his accusers, he must be disciplined.

The purpose of discipline is the healing and reconciliation of all concerned and for the glory of God. When the accused refuses to be accountable before a fair court of the Body, it becomes right to make that known. The ultimate penalty is disfellowshipping.

It is important to emphasize that it is not wrong to share the information and conclusions of a fair court. If the brother or sister does not repent, it is Scripturally required that the sin and discipline be made known. Incredible as it might seem, some are so confused about these issues that they would consider the sharing of the decision of the court to be slander! Once due process has been followed, it is not slander. Instead it is a true but sad report that sometimes must be given to restore the Body to health and to cut off the unrepentant. At times even the repentant must support the sharing of the report of the court. We may need to rebuke a leader publicly – that all might fear. Paul said some very negative things about some who were false and betrayed the gospel. We need only mention Alexander the coppersmith in this regard, per 2 Timothy 4:14 (NIV) – *"Alexander the metalworker did me a great deal of harm. The Lord will repay him for what he has done."*

Condemning or Narrow Attitudes

Wrong attitudes are another hindrance to justice. Most matters of sanctification are ultimately between the individual and God. Yes, counsel and discipline are important, but only the work of the Spirit transforms. When we speak of justice and discipline, we are speaking of enforcing standards of doctrine and behavior that are the historic and unifying positions of the Body. These standards are clearly outlined in the Scriptures. Some would initiate the process of Matthew 18 and bring a case for every little thing. Some are so under the spirit of legalism that they enjoin harsh discipline for minor doctrinal and behavioral matters. These legalistic groups give discipline a bad name. They cause reactions and further anarchy.

A Wrong Concept of Forgiveness

A wrong understanding of forgiveness has been a major cause of the destruction of justice in the Body. Forgiveness basically means to release another from further indebtedness. When a person says, "I was wrong. Will you forgive me?" the example of Jesus requires us to forgive! This forgiveness may require that restitution be made by the offending party to prove real repentance – the fruits of repentance.

To say, "I'm sorry," can be a cheap way for a person to continue in sin and be indulged by others. The manipulator will take full advantage of that. On the other hand, if the person is truly repentant and the issue is not one of a sin pattern, the offended party may release him from restitution. In either case, the motive of the offended party should be love.

The court of elders, however, should decide what is just and declare it. Then the offended party may make a choice. "Yes, I forgive you, but I do expect that if you are sincere, you will replace the car you took without permission and totaled in an accident because you were drinking." Or, "Yes, I forgive you, and because I know you are sincere and this is not a pattern, I want to release you from any responsibility to make restitution." The court should advise when release from restitution is detrimental to the person who sinned and to the honor of the name of God. Releasing a person, who un-Scripturally divorced and remarried, from child support is not right for the children, the spouse, or the one who divorced.

The Scriptural principle of forgiveness requires us to give up personal hurt and the desire for revenge. We must be free from desiring the other person to be hurt because we were hurt. The motive of personal revenge knows no limits. The offended party often is hurt beyond the normal reaction to the offense. That proves the offense tapped into the stored-up bitterness of a life of real or imagined offenses. No repentance or restitution can ever be adequate for such a one. In the Middle East, a single killing means that the offended one will take revenge and wipe out a whole clan. Hatred can be a way of life.

The principle of forgiveness requires us to seek to receive the ability that comes from God so that we can fully restore our fellowship with the one who did wrong to us. Our identification with the cross is a key to receiving the power to forgive. Forgiveness does not require that we trust. Trust is something to be given to the trustworthy. Trustworthiness is proven over time. Forgiveness does require that we love and fellowship again, and we should take small steps of trust to allow trust to be built.

How often must we give such forgiveness? Jesus says *seventy times seven* in Matthew 18:22. In other words, the truly repentant brother or sister is to be received back again and again without limit. As a counselor who has worked with severely troubled people – psychotics, schizophrenics, etc. – I have seen that being received is often necessary as part of their healing. They will sin again and again until the love and grace of God finally breaks through and delivers them. All of that has to do with what I call *forgiveness as a transaction*.

However, what if the person does not repent and has no desire to make restitution? Must we forgive anyway *and* act like nothing happened? I have three answers to this question. No! No! No! If the person has sinned greatly, a loving brother must hold him accountable. To let one "off the hook" is to encourage him in further sin. We are commanded to, and thus responsible for, correcting a brother or sister in sin, as we read Galatians 6:1 (NIV) – *"Brothers and sisters, if someone is caught in a sin, you who live by the Spirit should restore that person gently. But watch yourselves, or you also may be tempted."* We are to follow the due process of Matthew 18 if the sin is serious enough to require discipline. Truly, love does cover a multitude of sins in the ordinary course of life where we say the inappropriate thing or do something short of perfect love, etc. However, in matters of gross sin, for love's sake we must not let the brother "off the hook." The principle of forgiveness does not mean "business as usual." It may require people who know of a due process decision of disfellowshipping to separate from the disciplined person. Forgiveness, as a transaction between the sinner and the one grossly sinned against, cannot take place unless there is repentance. Acting in love does not mean we are called to act friendly in a "business as usual" way, as if there is nothing wrong.

Some will be shocked to read this. It goes against what has recently become popular teaching. The old humanistic indulgence returns under the guise of, "You must forgive me." Some lost people, like con artists, have claimed to be members of the Body in order to literally "rip off" the saints, secure in the fact that the saints must forgive and take no action. Is that really so? The saints can disfellowship the rogue and take him to court so that society is protected.

Don't we have to forgive? I believe there is another meaning to forgiveness which is different from the transactional meaning. This forgiveness does not restore our fellowship with the sinning brother. However, it puts our hearts right. When we say "I forgive" in this sense, we mean the following:

1) I free myself by the power of God from all bitterness, hate, and vengeful motives toward the brother. I receive this ability through the cross of Jesus.

2) Release the offender to God so that it is no longer a matter of my mental preoccupation and a hindrance to my joy in God. If the person will not be accountable to due process in the congregation, or due process is impossible because of the substandard situation of the Body, I need not have my life ruined by another's sin.

3) Receive love and compassion for the offender. My heart and prayer for the offender is for him to be fully redeemed or restored. Therefore, in compassion, I desire that the person come to true repentance.

4) Because my heart is loving, if the person repents, I will fully receive him back in the transaction of forgiveness.

This definition is a different but related meaning of forgiveness. It is *forgiveness as an attitude of love and compassion toward the offender.*

However, we must not be accomplices by encouraging people to sin. Some teach a forgiveness that would do just that and allow the one in sin to minimize the seriousness of sin. Casting out the unrepentant sinner in First Corinthians 5 had the effect of awakening him to the seriousness of his condition. It brought real repentance. Indulgence through the wrong concept of forgiveness can be a factor in the destruction of another.

Forgiveness in either sense is not easy. A wife whose husband had fallen into adultery must overcome great personal hurt to receive compassion. Even when he repents, the transaction of forgiveness is not easy. This forgiveness means that the past offense would no longer be brought up in times of conflict.

Forgiveness does not mean that we give up our quest for a justice motivated by love and for the good of all.

The Assumption of Moral Equivalency

Assuming moral equivalence seems to be another major problem of modern people. In foreign affairs, the government that commits the worst atrocities is made equivalent to the one with imperfections. The Gulag the Soviet Union, a huge evil, was equated with the jailing of Puerto Rican terrorists in the United States. These terrorists set off bombs that killed the innocent to achieve a national independence which the majority of Puerto Ricans did not want! Yet leftists spoke of both situations as equal evils.

In situations of discipline, the argument of moral equivalence is often heard as a reason not to seek justice through due process or not to follow the concluding judgment of a fair process. For example, suppose a leader grossly slanders another leader. The innocent leader suffers years of discrediting in a concerted disinformation campaign. He has not been able to get the offenders to adhere to any fair process for resolution. In frustration, he lets the cat out of the bag that he believes the others are in sin. He calls for due process but few will stand with him on this principle. Someone is always nearby to say something like, "Well, how can we claim they are in such sin? I have heard you speak negative things about them." This is an example of assuming moral equivalence. All parties are not equally to blame.

While every person must fully repent of their sin, there are few cases where both parties are each 50% at fault. If one party is only 5% guilty in a conflict, he must fully repent for his 5%. Yet that does not mean both sides are equal in the dispute – or morally equivalent. The other party will need to fully repent for their 95% responsibility in a situation!

Often people assume that if there is a conflict, both parties must be equally to blame. Israel must be equally to blame for the lack of peace in the Middle East despite the wars started by the Arab nations. In my experience, it is very unusual to find moral equivalency in disputes. Usually one party is far more to blame than the other. However, there are some situations that are exceptions to this rule.

Scriptural injunctions enjoin us to submit major disputes to fair judgment. All must have a fair day in court in order that testimony and investigation might disclose the truth. Perhaps one or both parties will have to repent of various sins and make restitution (to the Body at large, if not to each other). However, the assumption of moral equivalency destroys the possibility of justice. Until there is due process in a fair court, we do not know that there is moral equivalency at all. The one who refuses to submit to due process is guilty of sin; there is no moral equivalency in this case. Almost invariably, the one who is willing to submit to a fair, process of evidence and judgment is the one in the right. Again, there are exceptions.

Let us repent of the desire to be liked by all. Let us repent of all false teaching that leads us to *assume* moral equivalence between parties to a dispute. Yes, we are all imperfect. However, our imperfect actions are not the same as gross sin. Our imperfections do not mean we are on the same plane as one who is in gross sin, nor does imperfection disqualify us from pursuing the injunctions in Matthew 18:15ff.

The Wrong Definition of Taking Up an Offense

In Psalm 15:3 (KJV) we read that one of the characteristics of a righteous man is that he is one who does not *"taketh up a reproach* [offense] *against his neighbor."* Note that other translations are different, yet the teaching derived from this verse goes something like the following: "If someone does something wrong to someone else, it is between them. It should in no way affect my relationships. Therefore, I must continue to relate to them in the same way. This interpretation of "not taking up an offense" counsels neutrality in every controversy. Yet this interpretation is not the meaning of the prohibition and is contrary to other clear Scriptural texts.

First, taking up an offense means being bitter in spirit on behalf of another person because it is perceived that that person was wronged. This bitterness and offense is manifested, in a milder form, in distancing oneself from the one who committed the wrong. In a more severe form, it shows in speaking against the other who supposedly did the wrong. Sometimes that happens when the person himself who was supposedly wronged does not feel wronged or offended! The person who takes up the offense usually does so because of unhealed hurt and bitterness from the past. This past hurt is tapped into by more recent events and by their interpretations of those events. *Wrongly taking up an offense should be defined as becoming angry and bitter at one who supposedly did wrong without a righteous attempt to handle the problem according to Scriptural due process.* The heart is wrong whenever it is given to hurt and bitterness. The correction of a person in the wrong should always be motivated by compassion.

In the Scriptural order, sins committed publicly can be corrected by any mature brother or sister. If the sins are serious, it is judicious for elders to bring correction. Private wrongs should be handled by the offended party. Unless that person first sought to correct the one in sin, no one else should know about it. If such an attempt fails, then, according to Matthew 18, two or three others can be made a part of the process. Therefore, the one who takes up an offense in an un-Scriptural manner either should not even know about it and has been part of a gossip transaction, or is not willing to be part of a redemptive solution to a public wrong. It is certainly wrong to take up an offense for one who will not deal directly with the one who did the wrong. Much gossip and sin in the Body is a result of gutlessness! In no case should there be gossiping or dealing with matters non-covenantally outside of due process.

However, when one was sinned against seriously, and when the one who sinned refuses to repent or be part of God's order for resolving disputes (such as being unwilling to submit to fair judgment in disputes), we are duty bound to stand with the one who is willing to do right. Doing so may require separating from the one unwilling to seek reconciliation in a Scriptural way. That is the clear teaching of Matthew 18:15ff, 1 Corinthians 5:11ff, as well as Isaiah 59 on the role of the intercessor standing with integrity and justice.

Contrary to popular opinion, Scripture requires us to stand with the one grossly violated, with the one denied justice, and to separate from the one who refuses to act according to Scriptural norms of justice and due process. Doing so is not taking up an offense in the way precluded by the Scriptures. This separation is to occur only when attempts at due process fail. It is to be done for love's sake, not for bitterness, revenge, or other such base motives. If we would understand that and so act, we would see much of the gross sin in the Body addressed and handled. We could take a giant step toward cleaning up our act. To not stand against evil in this way is to empower people in their evil. It is to allow satan to maintain his hold on the life of the one sinning.

Fear of Shepherding

One of the hindrances to justice and discipline is the fear of shepherding, which I prefer to call "over-lordship." I refuse to have

Scriptural words stolen because some people misused the words and gave them un-Scriptural meanings. Shepherding is indeed a positive word in the Scriptures. Per over-lordship, anarchy is not the answer. We live in a lawless age that does not respect authority. Additionally, it is not over-lordship to have structures for congregational discipline, to enforce Scriptural standards for members and leaders, to seek counsel and confirmation from mature members of the Body before making significant decisions before God, and to disciple new members of the Body. That is simply historic, Scriptural teaching. Theology formed in overreaction to error is bad theology.

What is over-lordship? It consists in setting up an order of government in which the leader comes between a person and God so that the right of personal decision before God is precluded. That can be done overtly by the leader's asking to be followed as *the* voice of God to the follower. It also can be done by making social ostracism the price of going in directions contrary to leadership advice. An individual ultimately must be free to find the will of God for himself within the boundaries of Scriptural teaching on right and wrong. As part of God's order and wisdom, importance is placed upon getting counsel and confirmation, along with moving forward together. Yet every person must ultimately weigh all counsel in his own closet of communion with God. People will stand before God for their decisions, in regard to what the Spirit says. It is our duty to see that structures of counsel, leadership, and community do not compromise the principle of the individual's decision, in conscience, before God. We can require of another only what Scripture commands.

Over-lordship seeks to determine personal directions for the sheep's life rather than provide oversight and encouragement. Over-lordship penalizes the member for not following advice which, although it may be good, is not a Scriptural command. It violates the principle of the person's responsibility to hear God's direction by the counsel of the Spirit given in the inner man.

The issue of over-lordship is sometimes raised as a smoke screen by those who do not want to be accountable in a Scriptural way. Thus the lack of justice in the Body is often due to a fear of accountability. They resist the Scriptural injunctions of accountability, enforcement of standards, discipleship training, and discipline. Such a smoke screen must not be allowed to obscure the fact that Scriptural justice is commanded for the Body, and the fact that the issue of over-lordship is really a very different issue. Of course, extreme over-lordship is a serious error that should be disciplined! On the other hand, there can be strong authority structures that do not violate the Scriptures. There is also room for different structures of government within the Scriptural framework of due process and justice.

What is Mature Accountability?

The purpose of authority is not to exercise over-lordship in the lives of the sheep. In its normal functioning, leadership is to equip the saints for the work of ministry. Everyone is called to some form of service. However, it is up to the sheep to submit for training and to respond to the Spirit concerning their calling. Beyond minimal standards of membership, it is up to the sheep to decide the level of involvement. Of course, leadership has the right to refuse a person who desires to undertake an area of ministry in the Body if the leaders believe that the person is unprepared for it. It is not wrong to remove someone from full "membership in good standing" for failing to fulfill basic membership standards of attendance, tithing, etc. However, when such is done, it is cause for exhortation, not for disfellowshipping. Transfers to other groups should make clear that the person's not being in good standing dealt with membership standards and not gross sin or error on other levels. Perhaps the new group will offer membership because it has different standards or will exhort the person to fulfill standards there.

Although leaders have the right to order the life of the corporate congregation, and the sheep do not have the right to minister contrary to this ordering, the shepherds of the flock have no right to dictate the personal life direction of the members. Shepherds are only to counsel and confirm in personal, directional areas. They should affirm people in their consciences when they disagree with the leadership. One can affirm conscience without confirming a decision.

Our concern for discipline is not a call for over-lordship. It is merely to enforce discipline in areas of sin that Scriptural teaching designates as gross sin or doctrinal error. Mature leadership is strong where gross sin and error are concerned, but always with the goal of restoration. Mature leadership is motivated by redeeming love. Mature leadership offers leeway to the members in regard to other issues. Mature leaders hold other leaders accountable to basic standards, but they release them to creatively pursue the voice of God in their areas of ministry.

Narrowness in Moral and Doctrinal Standards

Some have distaste for all teaching on due process, discipline, and justice because the history of the Body sometimes reveals a lack of wisdom in their application that is due to legalistic and doctrinal narrowness. Pre-tribulationists disfellowshipped the post-tribulationists. Today, without due process, pre-millennialists separate from amillennialists. In the nineteenth century, the closed brethren disfellowshipped the open brethren because they allowed non-brethren members of the Body to share in the Lord's Supper. Indeed, the Nazarenes in the early twentieth century disfellowshipped the early Pentecostals. Speaking in tongues was considered to be of the devil and thus a level of offense that called for disfellowshipping. All this discipline has caused a reaction and moved many toward total non-discipline in the Body today!

The solution for severe doctrinal disagreements among those who profess the confession of classical Scriptural orthodoxy is not to disfellowship. It is to pray and seek the Lord to see if we first can be given the heart to see in the same way. If we cannot, and the disagreement is severe, we should separate in an amicable way. It is helpful to disclose the reasons. God is not pleased with our need to separate like Paul and Barnabas, but He is less pleased with our disfellowshipping one another over offenses that are not Scripturally defined as major ones. We can cooperate in significant ways and distance ourselves without slandering and disfellowshipping. Birds of a feather, after all, will flock together. However, within the bounds of Scriptural orthodoxy, God calls for greater love and mutual acceptance.

There will be narrow groups. Human pride will always tend to legalism, to adding to God's standards, and to man-made laws. For example, the groups that disfellowship others who do not endorse the King James Version as inerrant will be a side eddy in the last days. Human pride also will tend to anarchy. But that is no reason for us not to enjoin what Scripture requires. The historic and broadly understood Scriptural standards for membership and leadership should be established in our midst. A true manifestation of God's order is the best safeguard against the extremes of both legalistic narrowness and anarchy.

Severe discipline should be applied only in cases of gross doctrinal or moral error, as clearly defined by the Scriptures, which I do believe are clear in its standards. In addition, the history of the Body reveals a consensus for understanding these standards of the Scriptures.

Congregational Courts

A congregational court is a human, though divinely mandated, institution. It can err, and it can only be as good as the humility, wisdom, and spiritual maturity of the elders of the court. Therefore some have concluded it is better to leave all judgment to God. He will directly judge. Of course, such a thought is directly contrary to the Scriptural statements already presented in this book. Indeed, the same argument could be used against our civil courts. That would be disastrous in society, and it is disastrous in the Body. It is a prescription for anarchy.

On the other hand, it is better to have courts that make errors than to have no courts at all. God will raise up the truly humble and righteous if there is misjudgment. It should be noted that only serious sin and doctrinal error should come to such court situations.

Additionally, there are safeguards that can mitigate unfair judgment and invalid disfellowshipping. I have had direct experience with such errors. In these cases, the fact that there is a plurality of denominations, independent congregations, and apostolic networks is a safeguard against the abuse of the principles of congregational discipline. Yet all should seek to deeply honor the principles of discipline and to support legitimate discipline wherever possible. We at least should respectfully seek the facts and documentation for all discipline situations that involve us. God, with other ministerial flows in the Body, can vindicate one who was falsely judged. That is better than having no judiciary and waiting for God's supernatural judgment!

The one who refuses to pursue justice through due process, when they have been seriously sinned against or if there is a serious sin against the Body, violates a Scriptural norm. If a person accused will not submit to a process of judicial decision, then the rest of the Body should stand with the offended party. We should separate from those who will not resolve issues through due process. Otherwise they are encouraged in sin and empowered to continue doing evil. On the other hand, a party who claims to be offended but who will not submit his claim to fair judgment should not be believed, nor should his report be received if the other party is willing to submit to Scriptural norms. He should be confronted to handle his accusations Scripturally according to Matthew 18.

To establish God's law on a basic level among His people requires that we adopt explicit and implicit Scriptural norms in several areas. To enforce these norms, we must establish congregational courts, understand and adopt Scriptural standards for leaders and members, and remove members and leaders who no longer fulfill these standards.

That the believing community does not rise up and demand Scriptural standards shows how far we are from the knowledge of God's ways. The words of the Psalmist are appropriate for our day in Psalm 119:136 – *"Rivers of water run down from my eyes, because men do not keep Your law."* Earlier, the same writer noted with great sadness in Psalm 119:126b – *"For they have regarded Your law as void."*

John 17:21 Wrongly Applied

In a most glorious passage, Jesus prayed for His followers to be one as He and the Father are one. An incredible amount of "sloppy agape" (false love which is not love at all) has come from wrong interpretations of this verse, especially in the charismatic movement and the liberal, ecumenical congregations. There is a sense that, if we are to be one, all who profess to love Jesus are to be accepted. Among charismatics, those who claim to speak in tongues are given more of a free pass. We are to overlook all doctrinal issues and indulgently forgive moral wrong, even if not repented of. Out of this broad-hearted unity, it is thought, revival will come. What incredible rubbish! Will the Holy Spirit really come in revival for that which is full of sin and unholiness? Jesus did not pray that we would be one in an ecumenical salad, seasoned with gross sin and doctrinal error. Of course, we must overcome the barriers of narrowness and legalism to be one. However, Jesus prayed that we would be one as He and the Father are one. That is the oneness of a holy people who clearly affirm the great doctrinal truths that were once and for all delivered to the saints. That the verse of John 17:21 is used to thwart Scriptural justice standards and discipline in the Body is almost incredible and certainly tragic.

We live in a day in the Body in America when there is a wholesale departure from historic standards that once prevailed in evangelical Protestantism, including early Pentecostalism. This fact prompts us to ask the question of whether or not we have discovered something that was not known in the historic faith. Have we discovered a new meaning to liberty and forgiveness in the Messiah whereby the minister, having committed adultery, can continue in leadership? Have we really discovered a more wonderful meaning for grace? I do not believe so. Rather, I believe this departure reflects the general lawlessness in our society and the lowering of standards everywhere. The Body now reflects the world system and, like Hollywood, has its own version of "beautiful people" who are exempt from normal morality. There always have been lawless men and women claiming special revelation by which they could lead the people of God astray. One needs only to mention Thomas Muntzer of Luther's day. However, just as media experts dress up political candidates to deceive the public, so too they make Christian celebrities of renegades.

May this discussion of hindrances move the Body toward greater standards of love and justice.

CHAPTER 5

Accountability and Liberty

To be a healthy expression, there must be clear processes in place for congregational courts and the enforcement of their rulings. This clearly implies that we need to establish the meaning of jurisdiction. Jurisdiction defines where a person or leader is accountable. Jurisdiction defines the realm of the authority of a judiciary or a group of ruling elders. The discipling process should educate each one in these principles.

As for leaders, no one ever outgrows accountability to human representatives of God's law. The teaching that a man in a head leadership position is accountable only to God is an evil and false teaching that has produced great destruction and division. A leader may have a headship role, but accountability to mature peers is necessary if standards of due process and standards of evidence from Matthew 18 are to be carried out. Failure to fulfill standards in 1 Timothy 3 requires removal. One who falls into a deception of gross sin or doctrinal error is likely in pride and unlikely to remove himself. Therefore to protect the sheep, no one may ever set up structures that prevent their own removal, were they to become disqualified.

Defining Jurisdiction

The principle of jurisdiction does not require a particular form of congregational government. Many types of government allow jurisdiction and accountability to be established. The principle of jurisdiction does not require a centralized denomination. It can be carried out from a structure as centralized as an episcopal system (governance by overseeing bishops who are mutually accountable in a college of bishops), to one as decentralized as an independent congregation.

The primary judiciary in the New Testament is the eldership of the local congregation. Its jurisdiction extends to those who are part of the local flock and to those who are, or might be, affecting this local flock. This extension of jurisdiction is clear from the commandments to the elders of the local flock to guard the sheep from wolves and to exhort, teach, and rebuke the sheep.

Every citizen of our nation is under the jurisdiction of the courts established in the land. No citizen is ever beyond the jurisdiction of the courts in his local area and the special courts that handle special issues (e.g. tax courts). In the same way, every member of the Body comes under the jurisdiction of the congregational courts. Eldership is responsible for lovingly encouraging, teaching, counseling, and correcting. This same eldership is responsible for enforcing discipline in cases of severe covenant violation. This concept is no new thought; it was the historic position of the Body.

The Body in America often does not understand the principle of jurisdiction, contributing to an "anything goes" mentality amongst members of the Body. Note that many para-churches do not establish the nature of their jurisdictions. Likewise, many people find ways to fall between the cracks of jurisdictions. Despite these problems, most members of the Body are plainly to be under the jurisdiction of a local congregation's elders. It is also crucial that the elders are trained in their judicial responsibilities in addition to their other functions.

Membership

In the New Testament, jurisdiction under eldership is established by baptism. In today's society, such jurisdiction needs to be made clear before baptism. A type of formal membership needs to be established. Without it, the civil government will not uphold the right of congregations to discipline. Losing huge lawsuits could result from not establishing membership standards and then trying to enforce discipline. This situation has already been tested in court. Members need to clearly join and then be informed of their rights and the processes of discipline to which they are submitting.

What Are Basic or Minimal Standards?

The question, "What are basic or minimal standards?" concerns what we affirm to be Scriptural standards. What are minimal standards for membership and for leadership? A group may have higher standards than these minimal ones and might discipline on that basis. Those members who join make a covenant on the basis of those standards. Every group should make its standards clearly known. A group whose standards are less strict will not uphold another group's discipline on standards that are not shared. However, in shared areas, they should uphold one another. I am proposing here that congregations agree on historic, minimal standards without which they cannot claim to be Scriptural.

Minimal Standards for Members

I believe that baptism usually should constitute provisional membership (see Appendix V and VI). A minimal amount of instruction beforehand is adequate for ascertaining whether or not people are genuinely committing their lives to the Lord. If they are, it is not difficult to explain that a new person is, in baptism, joining the company of members under the local eldership. The new person can transfer later to any legitimate congregation, if he or she so desires. It should be understood that when one commits to Jesus, he commits to the Body of the Messiah and to the spiritual oversight of elders. This was understood in the first century. Baptism was joining the faithful community of the city under its elders; it was an initiation rite of entrance into the community before community witnesses. Because our concepts of spirituality are so individualistic, the truth of this process has been lost to many. I believe we would see more solid conversions and much quicker discipleship if this pattern was followed. We would see baptism as a real key to testing the prayer of receiving Jesus. *In baptism, we commit to Jesus as Lord and to the pattern of life taught in the Scriptures.*

A true conversion is life-changing. If there is no change, the conversion is questionable at best. Historic denominations always asked the person to give testimony of how his or her life had changed as evidence of true conversion.

A true member is one who meets minimal standards of membership: not engaging in a pattern of gross sin, confessing true Scriptural orthodox doctrine in its classical sense, and committing to congregational life. Different communities may have additional, specific standards. The latter could include tithing, agreeing with the basic ministry thrusts of the community, being a regular attender of essential gatherings, and serving in some area of Kingdom service.

A person may fall from membership standards (even backslide) without being in gross sin or doctrinal error. That would cause him or her to become a suspended member or a "member not in good standing." In this case, pastoral involvement is expressed in encouragement toward a more serious Scriptural lifestyle or in encouragement to transfer to another congregation where the person could be more committed. Perhaps the present congregation just does not fit that person. Counseling should encourage the person to be committed somewhere. Perhaps temporary circumstances are holding the person back. Such situations demand our prayers, love, and support. Our resources and time should be committed toward restoring.

Slipping from membership standards does not necessarily require disfellowship. To disfellowship is justified only when gross doctrinal error or sin requires it. To accept one as a member of the Body in such a case discredits the gospel. If people do not profess to be members of the Body, we are on different grounds and can relate to that person so as to win them to the Lord. The Body is a place for struggling saints, not just perfected saints. Therefore we need to bear with those who fall from membership standards (short of gross sin) and pray, counsel, and exhort them toward full commitment.

The discipline of repentance and restoration, repeated over and over in the context of forgiveness, usually produces motivation to not go through it again. The repentant thief becomes tired of restoring what was stolen plus twenty percent! The slanderer will desire to stop gossiping, for his repentance and restitution greatly humbles him; all those he spoke to are contacted concerning this sin of gossip and slander and asked for forgiveness! The one who falls into serious fornication may show restitution by his willingness to embrace a discipline that shuns situations hard for him to deal with until deliverance and the cross fully take effect.

Leadership Standards

The standards for elders and deacons in 1 Timothy 3 and Titus 1 are essential. Failure to meet these standards should preclude one from ordained leadership and governing roles. A continuous inability to live up to these standards should cause a person of integrity to voluntarily step down. If his peer leaders become aware of his failure to meet these standards, he should be asked to step down. If he is unwilling, he should be required to do so. We note that the standards of 1 Timothy 3 are based on relational success, which is based on character. No perceived measure of anointing should supersede these standards. Anointing can be used in witnessing and in non-leadership ministry contexts. God is serious about these standards because we reproduce what we are. Healthy leadership families reproduce in the community. (Leaders who are single should meet the relevant criteria in these New Testament chapters.)

The nature of gross sin shows why fallen leaders need to be removed from leadership. Gross sin is not just a chance happening. There are almost always roots that can be as serious as the sins, including loneliness, discouragement, an unhappy family life, unbelief, lack of intimacy with God or people, financial pressures, and more. Unless these roots are dealt with, the sin is likely to repeat itself. A group of capable leaders should oversee a process of counsel and restoration. When they are confident of the person's healing and character stability, restoration to leadership is possible. *It is not loving to allow the fallen leader to continue in leadership after a profession of repentance.* When there is no repentance, any sin which would require disfellowshipping should also require a significant period of restoration for the repentant leader. It is an obvious implication of the character standards for leadership in the Scriptures.

Scripture requires that such sin be dealt with publicly. Doing so protects the flock and enables them to fear God. They know that leaders are required to live up to Scriptural standards. It engenders confidence. Furthermore, it protects the person from future discrediting if, after restoration, he resumes leadership. It can hurt the ministry when past skeletons, which once were hidden, are later revealed. I know of instances where leaders stepped down and were restored, but later on someone discovered the sin and publicized it. What is publicly known does not discredit a person with most people of good will, when proper repentance and restoration took place. However, when a person's resume does not tell of the matter, some feel betrayed that they were not told; others lose trust. Gordon McDonald, the former head of InterVarsity Christian Fellowship, followed this right pattern. He ministers today with great credibility and is a credit to Scriptural principles of forgiveness and restoration. I firmly believe that any significant public ministry in the five-fold ministries is subject to the principles of the requirements in 1 Timothy 3.

Financial Support

One reason ministers who fall refuse to leave the ministry is the lack of loving financial support. Many ministers have a support base in congregations; other ministers have built up a support base constituency through years of service. They do not see any way they can adequately support their families were they to step down. They are not trained for other professions. Some would say that such ministers lack faith. That is callous. At such a time, faith is often at a low ebb. That is where the love of the Body is so important. There needs to be a financial support base to make up the difference during the time of restoration – or to enable a transition to another profession if the leaving of full-time ministry is to be permanent or long term. I believe a local congregation can, at the least, continue a part-time salary for a year. Congregations should cooperate to establish funds for this purpose. Otherwise many will choose to continue in ministry out of a sense of necessity to support their families. That is wrong. It is also wrong if the congregation does not lovingly support its fallen but repentant ministers. If the congregation is serious about enforcing standards, they also need to be serious about the compassion that is part of restoration.

Divorce and Remarriage

Standards required for members and leaders that concern divorce and remarriage are a source of great controversy today. Congregations, associations, and denominations are not united on what constitutes

Scriptural standards for divorce and remarriage. We are not united on whether or not a restoration to leadership is appropriate for one who has either a legitimate or an illegitimate divorce and remarriage. Indeed, many congregations do not recognize their responsibility to issue a letter or certificate of divorce with the right to remarry if they do believe there are legitimate grounds for such.

Some denominations believe there are never grounds for divorce and remarriage. Thus they do not allow for any divorced and remarried leaders to be restored, even if the people were divorced and remarried before they became members of the Body. When someone who has been divorced and is remarried comes to another group from such a denomination, the new group needs to find out the circumstances of the divorce and remarriage.

Those groups that believe there are legitimate, Scriptural grounds for divorce and remarriage need to issue a clear policy statement to define these grounds. Then, when a case of legitimate divorce with the right to remarry according to their standards does arise, they need to issue a certificate of divorce detailing the grounds for issuing a certificate of divorce detailing the grounds for their decision. If they do not issue such a certificate, and there is a divorce and remarriage which leads to discipline, they need to issue a statement of the grounds of their discipline and document that due process was followed. This will enable various groups to be aware of the standards involved and the reasons for the elders' decision. It can enable others to make an informed decision as to what level, if any, they can be involved with the divorced and remarried leader or member according to their own standards. (In Rabbinic Judaism, binding and loosing is understood to include the responsibility of issuing a certificate of divorce when legitimate. This certainly is the implication of Matthew 18, with regard to the responsibility of eldership.)

All groups that seek to uphold Scriptural standards should be able to agree upon the need for any divorced person to step down from leadership, regardless of the reason for the separation or divorce. Even if one spouse initiated and received a secular divorce against the will of the other partner and against the standards of the congregation, the relatively innocent party should not remain in leadership. Why? Divorce is a traumatic experience. A person who has been divorced is in no condition to continue in leadership and certainly does not fulfill the family requirement standards of 1 Timothy 3. In my view, such a person may eventually requalify by these standards, either as a single person or in a new marriage. However, even if the divorced person is not in sin, he or she needs to requalify. That will take a significant period of time. Health reproduces health; the newly divorced cannot be in a good position for Scriptural leadership. It is amazing to me that such an obvious implication of Scriptural teaching is missed by so many in today's Body.

In regard to divorce and remarriage, the following Standards are held variously in the Body today.

1) There are no grounds for divorce with a right to remarry – ever. Therefore, to divorce and remarry in some groups leads to disfellowshipping, or at the least a permanent exclusion from leadership.

2) Divorce with the right to remarry is legitimate if a spouse is in unrepentant adultery, repeated adultery, homosexual sins or other gross sexual sins.

3) Divorce with the right to remarry is legitimate according to statement #2, as well as for desertion by a spouse according to First Corinthians 7. In such a case, the deserting spouse should be disfellowshipped.

4) Agreeing with statements #2-3, some add the following proviso: A divorce may be granted in exceptional cases where a spouse has abandoned the marriage in covenantal responsibilities, even though he or she continues to live in the same house. This type of divorce is very exceptional and should be handled with great care before the elders

grant it. The partner who abandoned the covenant should be disfellowshipped (sometimes wife-beating, drunkenness and other types of severe sin like rebellion, abuse, and psychological abandonment are included).

5) Some accept the grounds of #2-4, as well as the following: Though both marriage partners are members of the Body and try as best they can, if they simply cannot get along, it is better to divorce than to build up bitterness. God's forgiveness is such that these persons should be allowed to remarry.

This provides a brief summary of the various positions held. I do not see how any faithful disciple could come to the conclusion of #5 while taking Scripture seriously. Scripture makes it plain that two truly born again members of the Body always have the resources in God to make their marriage work, if they are willing. However, those who grant divorce for this reason, and there are some evangelicals who do, should make the grounds clear so that others can know where they stand.

Standards for divorce and remarriage should be part of the written policy of every congregation. The air can be cleared by issuing their standards and the grounds for specific decisions in divorces, with the documentation of due process. Then each group can decide how it will relate to the divorced person by its own standards, even if those standards differ from the group that originally issued the decision. In addition, a person can transfer later to a group with more lenient standards, if he so desires. Other groups can choose by their standards whether or not to receive such a person as a leader. At the least, knowing the truth of the matter helps us decide with clarity according to conscience. But today, great confusion reigns in this area.

Our community does not allow those who are, according to our standards, illegitimately divorced and remarried to be members or to minister among us unless there is full repentance and restoration according to our understanding of the Scriptures.

What about the person who divorced and remarried without Scriptural grounds? This area is one of the more difficult issues. Can the person be restored to membership? I believe it is possible, but only if repentance is real. Many statements show no repentance at all and negatively influence the quality of marriage commitment among the saints if allowed.

Recently a number of prominent leaders have fallen into the sin of adultery. Some have left wives and married their secretaries without having any Scriptural grounds for divorce and remarriage. Sadly, I have heard un-Scriptural statements of repentance. "Well, yes, it was wrong, but God knows our weaknesses and that I could not help it. I have asked His forgiveness and believe it is under the blood. We must be merciful if we are to have mercy. I simply came to the end of my rope and temptation overcame me. However, God is forgiving and knows I could not handle remaining with my former wife, and He knew that my new wife was the one I truly needed." This is not Scriptural repentance at all. We have even heard some say that Scripture must not be used legalistically, as the Spirit led them to divorce and remarry because God knew their call to be exceptional. Yes, we are to be merciful and not exact revenge, but for mercy's sake we need to uphold Scriptural standards because we reproduce what we are. Leaders who are immoral and indulge sin will produce a Body full of sin – without the fear of God and the power of God.

Compare the previous attempt at repentance with what a truly repentant leader would say: "My God, what have I done? I left my wife and married another woman. I brought disrepute upon the gospel. If I could do it again, I would not so sin. I had no excuse to do so, for I had the power of the Scriptures and the Spirit to overcome my test. If only I could do it over. I am stepping down from leadership. I do not know if I can ever be in leadership again. However, the teaching of Scripture now requires me to make the second marriage work. For the sake of the glory of God, however, I must step down. I will submit myself to my colleagues and to God that I might be of some use to Him in the future." That is repentance. It will surely be met forgiveness, but not necessarily with restoration to leadership.

What would restitution be in such a case? The proof would be repentance before the spouse and the children, responsible child support if children are involved, and a lifetime profession of the truth. This profession requires that the person never justify the action, rather to consistently profess to have missed God's will in the act of divorce and remarriage. Testimony to the grace of forgiveness is not wrong if it is in the context of such clear restitution. The profession of the truth is part of this restitution. By this truth, other couples will be motivated to work on their marriages when conflicts arise and to not easily bail out.

Doctrinal Differences

Although we are duty bound to take congregational discipline from other groups seriously, we are not required to simply accept every decision of discipline at face value. There are certainly variations in theology and experiential perspectives. For example, there are different teachings on what the Scriptures say per divorce (and other issues). It is helpful if the theology behind the judgment is made clear. This allows a person who was disciplined to freely join a group that would not have judged them on the basis of those standards. For example, in the Assemblies of God, a divorced person who remarries may never be restored to leadership. Another group, however, may believe in a process of repentance, counseling, restitution, and restoration that could restore that person to leadership. However, that situation should not cause division between the Assemblies of God and the group of the other persuasion – as long as both are clear on their differences and both seek to uphold other basic Scriptural standards.

The gifts of the Holy Spirit can also bring complexities into congregational courts due to different teachings and levels of experience of all involved. It would not be constructive for those do not believe in and practice the gift of prophecy today to be judging error in the exercise of prophetic gifts. Likewise, a charismatic would have a difficult time accepting the judgment of doctrinal error and disfellowshipping from a fundamentalist congregation where the decision was based on the view that exercising the gift of prophecy is wrong in principle and compromises the authority of Scripture. Similarly, it is not judicious for non-charismatics to judge an issue where someone is accused as a false prophet. Even the charismatic world has differences of theology concerning what would constitute a false prophet. These instances can lead to gross miscarriages of justice. Prophetic practices need to be judged by people of similar theological persuasion. Theological discussion among different communities is the prescription for differences of doctrine not defined in classical orthodoxy. Differences between Evangelicals, Charismatics, Pentecostals, Word of Faith people, etc. should not be decided by disciplinary courts!

False Restitution and Secular Courts

Most members of the Body do not understand that the Scriptural concept of repentance includes restitution, thus many have been hoodwinked by satan's emissaries. Many of the sins in the Body could be prosecuted in secular courts, but they are not due to Scriptural injunctions to not take a fellow member of the Body to the pagan courts. It is good that we do not go to the secular courts. Yet people are often received back into fellowship because they say "I'm sorry." One professional con artist, who professes to be a member of the Body – but is not – travels throughout the country to congregations and fraudulently "rips off" the saints. When caught, he says "I'm sorry." He has no intention of paying back his victims. He believes he has the saints over a barrel because, by his profession of being a member of the Body, they cannot take him to secular court. We are to be wiser than that. A congregational court needs to disfellowship him so that members of the Body may take him to the civil courts. Only if he proves his repentance by working on restitution can the Body accept him as a member. Again with Zacchaeus, he restored all that was stolen, and then Jesus announced that the Kingdom of God had come to his house!

A person who has grossly sinned needs to prove his repentance with fruit before being fully received back into fellowship. There can be a probationary acceptance until that repentance is shown to be real. The number of times a person may sin and repent in word and deed and be received back is not limited. Love may cover a multitude of lesser sins, but gross sins or capital offenses require a demonstration that the repentance is real. A loving community will do all it can to aid the individual in showing the reality of repentance, including prayer, hugs, encouragement, and even helpful direction in making the steps of restitution. However, significant steps of restitution must be made. Concerning membership, we affirm that restoration to the Body and to full fellowship is open to all, no matter what the sin.

Restoration

Can one who has grossly sinned be restored not only to membership but even to leadership? Can illegitimately divorced and remarried people be restored to membership and to leadership? If restoration is possible in such cases, what would constitute adequate repentance, restitution, and restoration? This question is a cause for great controversy between congregations. May God restore our unity!

Many use the "call of God" idea as grounds for not enforcing discipline. The call may well be there, but so must the character qualifications. That call must wait for the more important issues of character and for relational accountability to be established before entering back into the call.

Generally, truly repentant people desire to do all they can to right the wrongs they committed. They work to restore the reputation that was slandered, and they seek counselling to restore a broken marriage. They repay stolen money plus additional compensation. However, there is no real consensus concerning the definition of restoration. Almost all believe that a person can be restored to full membership. God's unconditional love and forgiveness restores any truly repentant person. However, this love must not be construed as indulgence. It is not an "anything goes" philosophy.

Other than in the difficult area of interpreting passages on marriage and divorce, most would agree that God can restore anyone to membership and leadership no matter what the past sin. However, trustworthiness needs to be re-established. That often takes a number of years. If restoration takes place, the past cannot be covered up. Whether or not restoration to leadership is expedient for the sake of God's Kingdom is important as well. What is legally acceptable may not be expedient for God's Kingdom.

One of the greatest sources of division in the Body today is the receiving of disciplined leaders by a new group, thus thwarting the process of restoration. If a group's standards are less strict than the disciplining group, but still reasonably defensible in the light of Scripture, that can be made clear. A person under discipline who repented in word and deed may after a period of time desire to transfer to this other group. He should then be free to do so. However, a period of restoration should still be enjoined by the new group. Communication between the two groups is important. Standards of 1 Timothy 3 should be met in the context of the new group if the person is to return to leadership. If the standards of the two groups vary greatly, the group with stricter standards must decide, in conscience, what level of involvement they may have with the other group and the former leader. Two cannot walk together unless they agree. However, if there is no continuation in gross sin, the two groups can at least live amicably in the same area.

The Principle of Transfer

Jurisdiction is maintained over members by the eldership of a congregation where they are members until they are transferred and received in another Bible-believing congregation. I do not believe that it is correct for an individual to simply resign from membership. The exception to this rule is when the local congregation becomes cultic and will not transfer to a Bible-believing variety of congregations (Charismatic, non-Charismatic, Independent, Presbyterian, Methodist, Messianic Jewish, Free Church, Lutheran, etc.). If another group does not understand or practice the principle of transfer, the first congregation can maintain contact and some jurisdiction until the brother has joined the new group. The original group can contact the new group and seek to communicate in such a way that the new group will be aware whether a question of severe moral sin or error is at issue. Of course, no transfer to an unbelieving group can be blessed. In those cases, a congregation can then carry out their discipline, but they also must recognize their limits if the backslidden person joins a congregation in heresy or anarchy. Hopefully, through discipling, our membership will only want to join groups that practice the principles they share.

If jurisdiction and discipline are to have a more significant effect, it is crucial for congregations to respect the principle of transfer and to seek to uphold the discipline of the congregation wherever possible. Any member in good standing, or not in good standing as long as they are not under discipline for gross doctrinal sin or error, can and should be freely transferred. The witness of the Body is compromised, however, when for various reasons other congregations receive those who are under discipline for gross sin or error.

When people come to a congregation from another part of the Body, it is crucial for a leader who has authority to initiate communication with the original group. "Is there any reason we cannot receive the brother or sister?" If the issue is gross sin or error, the new congregation should seek documentation to establish that the first congregation acted with due process and clearly established the case. On the other hand, the new congregation can provide a check on unreasonable discipline by the first congregation. For example, "over-lordship groups" will disfellowship members for failing to obey the leaders in areas of a person's life direction, for failing to adequately tithe, or for other errors which are less than extreme. A new congregation usually should seek to uphold the discipline of the first, but is not bound to do so if the discipline is found to be unfair by Scriptural norms. The discipline of local congregations is to be respected, but is not absolute in a way that would establish tyranny.

It is important to destroy the competitive spirit between congregations. This spirit causes us to be too ready to believe the worst about another congregation and to believe a negative report from a new member who transfers. We should always seek the facts, even if the congregation is one which we do not trust. If to our knowledge a congregation is in decent order, and is a Bible-believing group, it may be wise to see if the reason for transfer is that significant. Perhaps a leader can restore people to their former congregation and help clear up problems. Imagine the trust and unity that would grow! Francis Frangipane, an Iowa pastor and leader in fostering unity in the Body, requires in most cases that a potential transferee return to his former congregation for at least one month. During this month, that person is to offer intensive, daily prayer for the pastor, leaders, and the congregation. Afterwards, if the potential transferee still desires to change congregations, Pastor Frangipane will work with the other congregation to ensure a healthy transfer.

It is obvious that the establishment of good relations among congregations of various denominations and apostolic flows is important and needs to be pursued. Good relations between congregations who care about integrity foster love and justice, while hastening the day of the Lord's return. It can lead to joint efforts among congregations for more effective evangelism and positive change in our communities, cities, counties, and states!

Appeal Process

I believe that it is very important for denominations and apostolic flows to provide at least one level of a court of appeal. The appeal court can decide whether or not there is sufficient evidence for an appeal to be heard. Cases that have significant trans-local implications can be heard here as well. This can provide stability and greater confidence in the decision of the lower court.

When issues arise between congregations or movements that are not in the same denomination, these issues can be handled in several ways.

1) Congregations of a locality may subscribe to an inter-congregational court to hear such issues. This court is composed of leading elders of the city who can deal objectively with these issues. Following this process could begin to restore a perception of us being part of one Body – the "church of the city."

2) An *ad hoc* court can be established to which both sides of the dispute submit. This court should be comprised of men of experience and wisdom who are trained in judicial responsibility. Both sides would agree to its composition.

3) There may be need for specialized courts for issues too difficult for elders trained under normal circumstances. Issues that deal with complex financial and legal matters

may require a group for mediation that understands these complex issues. The Christian Legal Society seeks to provide a court of arbitration for such issues. The elders responsible for the members involved should be fully aware of the proceedings and should be involved where they can in such cases.

Accountability in Inter-congregational Matters

There are also times when the disciplining of leaders is too hard for the local eldership, especially when people around the city are being impacted. My call for due process and accountability is particularly relevant for those who believe in *completely* independent, local congregations. Under an eldership, I do not believe that this type of congregation is the Scriptural ideal. Indeed, the Scriptural ideal is probably where congregations have such unity that they would be tied together in a "church of the city" eldership.

This "church of the city" eldership could handle inter-congregational (and inter-denominational) disputes. Cities could be linked to *ad hoc* groups; these groups could form to resolve disputes among congregations in various cities or regions. Leading fathers could serve in this way. However, the Body today is too diverse in doctrine and practice to make such ties totally practical at the present time. There are several other ways to link judicial concerns beyond a local congregation.

First, congregations may be linked officially in an association or denomination. Their bylaws can include a process for appeal and for handling disputes that are either too difficult for the local congregation or that have implications beyond the local congregation (such as removing a leader who has regional, national, or international influence). Congregations may also be linked by apostolic connections to a pastor of pastors, who can bring elders together for such inter-congregational concerns. Lastly, *ad hoc* councils may be formed that can judge issues beyond the ability of the local congregation. Such a council of leaders beyond the local congregation can be called together because relationships among leaders are healthy. Bylaws of the local congregation could specify the circumstances for, and the means by which, such a council would be called. My own preference is for an official linkage of autonomous, but not fully independent, congregations. However, because disciplinary matters sometimes affect other congregations in the same city, it is good to include representatives of other local congregations in those matters.

Para-church Organizations

Some para-church organizations enforce clear standards, and others by their structure allow for great abuse by the ministers who either lead them or are within them. Some organizations believe they should have judicial jurisdiction over their workers, and others do not. There are debates in the Body as to whether or not para-church organizations are Scriptural. In the New Testament, it appears that members of apostolic traveling teams were accountable primarily to the leadership of the team. However, that does not fit the structure of many of today's para-church organizations. I certainly do not wish to add fuel to the fire on the debate in this book. However, I do have some guidelines to suggest.

If the para-church organization is to be a source of jurisdiction in congregational discipline, it must have an eldership structure. This structure would be a board of real elders who can discipline and who have sufficient involvement in order to have real authority. If the organization decides not to enforce such discipline over its leaders and workers, then those who work in it must clearly be under the jurisdiction of local congregations. The jurisdiction should be made plain to every member of the organization as well as to the congregations connected to the workers. It then will be the responsibility of the para-church to uphold the discipline of the local congregations for its workers. On the other hand, if the para-church claims such jurisdiction, it should make that clear to all its workers when they join. Its elders should know their responsibility and fully embrace it. Local congregations should respect the discipline of the organization if standards of due process are followed. In this latter case, the para-church is really a kind of congregation with a specific mission. Local congregations should be informed of the nature of this jurisdiction.

If a para-church has a genuine board of elders to which it is truly accountable, I do not object to its having jurisdiction. However, that jurisdiction needs to be made clear. If leaders in both groups are trained in their judicial functions, these courts will be adequate for presumably 95% of the issues that arise.

Apostolic Teams and Authority

For those who believe that there is a continuing function for persons who perform apostolic functions (overseeing multiple congregations, pastoring pastors, directly planting new congregations, or indirectly aiding in the planting of new congregations), I desire to share some insight into the relationship of these people to what is being taught here per congregational courts. We do believe in apostles, with a small "a," defined as performing the functions previously listed.

In addition to local congregations, jurisdiction can be seen via trans-local ministries whose members are under the authority of the leadership of these apostolic teams. We believe that appeal courts under apostolic leaders can aid the cause of justice greatly when issues are between congregations. Furthermore, under joint apostolic leadership, appeal courts can be formed to handle disputes between flows of congregations. Actually, the reason a para-church can have jurisdiction Scripturally, in my view, is the Scriptures show members of apostolic teams as being accountable primarily to the team and not to a local congregation. In this case, however, the para-church is well served when overseen by a true plurality of elders who understand their function as an apostolic team responsible for its members. Although local congregations can minister to the needs of apostolic team members, it greatly eliminates friction for such para-churches to define and clarify jurisdictional boundaries. It also will aid local congregations where such team members attend. Scripturally, there is no para-church without eldership jurisdiction.

Every member of the Body is called to be under clear jurisdiction. That includes all leaders. Woe to those who call others to be accountable to them, but who are not accountable themselves. No one should connect to any organization that is so ordered.

Conclusion

Justice cannot be established in the Body today without due process and the restoration of congregational courts to handle such matters. That is one way wolves in sheep's clothing can be exposed and lose their influence. Unless the moral standards of the Body in the last days are high, we will be unable to stand firmly in the faith in times of battle. The breastplate is the breastplate of righteousness! Righteousness and justice are related concepts, stemming from the same Hebrew root word. Justice is simply the order of God's righteousness described by Scripture. That we are entering an age of intense tribulation is no excuse for avoiding these principles. The early fathers established congregational courts in the midst of great persecution and turmoil. I understand that God's restoration of the Body in the last days will produce a situation where greater prophetic knowledge and greater direct interventions by God will establish fear and holiness, such as in the case with Ananias and Sapphira. Direct intervention in judgment is not God's only method. As Paul needed to call for the establishment of congregational courts in 1

CHAPTER 6

Practical Instruction for the Body

Structure alone does not overcome problems. People of character in positions of leadership are necessary. On the other hand, leaders with great character can at times transcend inadequate structures of authority. This book makes it clear that Scriptural structure makes room for leadership to exercise gifting, but that leadership should never be without accountability. Checks and balances are part of the orientation of the Scriptures!

To fulfill the ideals of this book, several commitments are crucial for the entire Body to adopt. It is time for the charismatic movement in many quarters to repent for rejecting classical, historic standards because of a reaction against denominations. Denominations sometimes did develop centralized and stifling structures. However, the denominations also had many positives; not everything in the denominational structures was wrong. It is time for us to re-evaluate historic structures and ask questions of what is worthy to be fostered today. The anti-denominational stance of many comes from pride and leads to structures that are without justice or Scriptural order. The following are the commitments that the Body today needs to make to recover God's order of justice.

Commitment to Leadership Standards

It is time for the Body to commit to the leadership standards of 1 Timothy 3 and Titus 1. The only way discipline can be enforced is for each congregation and its leadership to commit to these standards and to set up structures of accountability whereby any leader who falls, and thus no longer fulfills these standards, can and will be removed.

Another part of establishing discipline requires those who are in traveling ministries and who are sent to establish new congregations or ministries to be truly accountable to an eldership of integrity. This group must be committed to the Scriptural standards for leadership and should vouch for the character and the adequate preparation of the minister covered. During the planting stage, these elders should hold the planter accountable to leadership standards and financial integrity. Until such time as a planter raises up elders in a new congregation, such channels of accountability should remain.

In New Testament times, recognized leaders gave letters of recommendation which were carried by traveling ministers. Can we do less today? It is time for the people of God to know the Scriptural standards for leadership and to make sure they are submitted to leaders who fulfill these standards. Doing so will be one significant check against authoritarian abuse. All members should know the proper way to bring charges against leaders who are in serious sin or error.

Commitment to Membership Standards

The need for minimal membership standards is crucial. A true seeker might not be living up to these standards. However, once he professes to be truly born again, he needs to be challenged to come into full membership. That can be done as part of baptism or shortly thereafter, when membership instruction has been given. A potential member needs to know his responsibilities as part of the congregation and his relationship to the elders of the congregation.

A congregation cannot allow one to profess to be a truly born again and yet live in gross sin or foster serious, basic doctrinal error. Secondly, to allow these people to remain connected to the congregation in a limited way, without real commitment, is to discourage the commitment of the whole community. It is time to build communities of faith that seek to reflect the Kingdom ideals taught by Jesus and by the apostles. It is time to stop building a weekly rally as a substitute for true life in the Body. A "McDonald's drive-in" religion is not Scriptural. A radio or television program is not a congregation!

Commitment to Establish Congregational Courts

The principle of the eldership in each local congregation having a judicial function needs to be firmly established. Congregations need to truly desire and pray that elders fulfill their full Scriptural function. The principle of congregational courts needs to be taught to the members. They also need to see what the eldership court is for and how it is to be used.

It is also important that courts be established to settle inter-congregational disputes where at all possible. At least local congregations can have provisions in their bylaws for ad hoc courts to be established for such disputes if they are not connected by denomination, apostolic flow, or congregational network to such a court of appeal. Courts of appeal are also a check against abusive structures of severe "over-lordship," which can develop in local congregations.

Commitment to Train Elders for Their Judicial Responsibilities

It is crucial for elders to be trained in their judicial responsibilities. Such training, first of all, would include understanding Matthew 18 and the Scriptural process of correction. It is also crucial for elders to be trained in clear knowledge of all the New Testament passages concerning their judicial function and of how to practically apply these passages.

It is important that elders be trained in Scriptural law and in how to apply it in the New Covenant order. All of the Scriptural instructions for judges and for the establishment of justice need to be fixed in the hearts of the elders. Elders need to learn how to weigh evidence and testimony. They need to be given practical examples of restitution that would fit various offenses. This training needs to fully examine the difference between Scriptural love and justice as compared to "sloppy agape." They need to know that rendering fair judgment, without favoritism, is a high Scriptural calling. Furthermore, they need to clearly understand that making a judgment on the basis of the evidence rather than simply calling for superficial reconciliation is very important. Eldership requires the fruits of the Spirit. Patience and wisdom are part of that judicial temperament that is necessary to the functioning of the congregational courts.

Elders also need to realize that they are responsible for issuing divorce certificates when justified and to refuse to issue when not justified. The penalty of congregational discipline should be used when a divorce without Scriptural justification is pursued. Indeed, an unwillingness to be reconciled to a spouse or to another member in good standing in the Body is grounds for discipline. The New Testament community is a community of forgiveness and reconciliation!

Commitment to Resolve Disputes

It is time for us in the Body to grow up. That means we are to seek to resolve our disputes in a spirit of love. Unless there are overwhelming convictions of conscience for separating from a community (or communities), we should submit to the decisions of the judiciary under which we are committed. Perfect justice and love are not to be expected in this life. Fostering wounded pride is sin and one of the greatest sources of division in the Body. Therefore we need a deeper commitment to carry out the decisions of the elders, rendered as part of the process of arbitration, instead of requiring a decision that fully confirms one's own position. We need to foster such deep commitment as highly valuable and only disobey when Scriptural principles are clearly violated. Commitment to avoiding splits is Scripturally enjoined. Unless there is gross moral sin or error in the leadership, the decisions of elders in resolving disputes should be accepted and submitted to for the sake of peace. Forgiveness, repentance, and restitution should be offered according to the wisdom of the elders' decisions. Even society, in general, requires a certain level of resolution before the civil courts of our land. Can we require less in the society of Jesus?

Of course, the disunity of today's Body concerning doctrinal matters means that disputes in many areas need to be judged by those who do not come from a vastly different doctrinal perspective. Although they come from vastly different perspectives, those who believe in the judicial function of elders would resolve some issues in the same way. These would be in areas of more universal doctrinal and moral agreement among people who believe in congregational discipline. However, many issues are not of this nature. Sometimes disputes arise that seriously divide people, even though the issues are not capable of clear determination by universally held norms of doctrine and behavior. In these disputes, judges need to share the basic theological thrust of the participants. It is important for judges to issue clear decisions that include their evaluation of the rights and wrongs in the situation. If they believe that minor issues are being given too much weight, they need to state the issues and the reasons that is so.

Commitment to the Principle of Disclosure

When leaders fall, there are feelings of hurt, confusion, disappointment, betrayed trust, and crises of confidence. The greater prominence a minister has correlates to how serious the fall becomes. We might also note that, to the extent a ministry truly makes a righteous impact, the more serious the attack of the devil to discredit the gospel.

How is confidence and faith restored? It is by making public the basic facts of the sin – not the lurid details. Also to be made public are the discipline that has been enjoined by those who hold the fallen leader accountable, along with the process for possible restoration. Public disclosure clears the air and restores confidence! It is so simple; why do so many not know it? Possible, not certain, restoration to leadership is in view because those who hold the leader accountable must affirm that standards of 1 Timothy 3 have been re-attained as a prerequisite to leadership. We believe in restoration for wounded and fallen soldiers. However, we believe in a process of restoration that reflects His principles. If sheep were wounded in the situation, both pastoral counseling and inner healing need to be available to the sheep.

Disclosure also has a reference to an open posture per notifying members of key governmental decisions. If members are to be included in the governmental process of the congregation, how much more should they be updated during difficult seasons? In general, congregants and constituents should know where funds are spent. They also should know the vision, direction, and policies of the organization through congregational gatherings, audited summaries that are accessible, written statements, etc. People who give should know that they are responsible before God to know to what they are giving. This knowledge must not be difficult for them to obtain.

Commitment to the Principle of Transfer

The world is full of professing but "Lone Ranger believers." They live contrary to Scriptural norms. It is crucial for every member of the Body to be established in the community of faith and to know to whom they are accountable. It is crucial for every leader to establish the same for his life. It is time for the Body to return to the historic standard of transfer as explained in the last chapter. These standards show the truth that all members of the Body are to be accountable and under elder jurisdiction. That jurisdiction remains until a person joins another congregation, apostolic flow, or team.

Summary

May God grant that these commitments become universal in the Body in the days to come. I believe these commitments are necessary if the Body is to mature and deal with the many wolves in sheep's clothing the enemy will send into our ranks in the last days. Fair processes of justice will protect the truly innocent and will ferret out the wolves.

CHAPTER 7

Illustrations Revisited

We now return to the illustrations from the first chapter and apply the principles that were discussed. The reader may want to review the illustrations from that chapter.

Illustration #1

The lack of shared, basic standards was a major weakness in the pastors' fellowships. For both this example and the next, I cannot too strongly emphasize that a pastors' fellowship should at least be based on minimum covenant standards. Such standards include: seeking to uphold the discipline of other congregations where such discipline adequately followed standards of due process; refusing to receive bad reports outside of a clear Matthew 18 process; and affirming a covenant of good report – which is crucial in such fellowships, otherwise they are easy prey for satan.

Of course, hindsight is easier than foresight. Therefore these next comments must be taken as offered with great empathy for Pastor Nelms, the leader of the fellowship.

In no way should the new pastor, Pastor James, or his pastor guest, Pastor Jacobs, have been allowed to share gossip and mistrust concerning the association of congregations to which Pastor Nelms was relating. Pastor Jacobs should have been cut off in his accusations and asked some pointed questions. With regard to his accusation of a hidden agenda, he should have been asked for proof of such. If he did not have any, he should have been rebuked for bringing his mistrust into the group. Secondly, his accusation of "over-lordship" should not have been allowed. Once that word had been mentioned, he should have been asked if he had sought to approach those leaders with evidence concerning over-lordship. If he had done so, then had he sought to approach them with other leaders? What was the nature of the evidence? Was the leadership group involved given a chance to answer their accusers face to face, with Pastor Jacobs as a witness? Or did Pastor Jacobs simply receive evil accusations against these leaders?

Those who leave a congregation sometimes make many unfounded accusations. However, when checked, most accusations fall to the ground. The devil is the great accuser of the brethren. It later came out that one accusation of "over-lordship" came from two men who were told they were to no longer share an apartment. They shared their anger at this intrusive shepherding. What they did not share was that they had a homosexual relationship which had come to light and was the cause for their discipline.

Illustration #2

The issue of a pastors' fellowship needing standards applies to this situation also. Our introductory comments for the first illustration apply here as well. However, the fact that evidence was presented to seven national leaders should have been sufficient cause for the pastors' fellowship to stand behind the discipline. The leader from New Hope Church who was under discipline had a national ministry. Therefore, it was not wrong to ask people with whom they were in relationship on a national level to confirm discipline.

On the other hand, the lack of local leaders in the discipline confirmation reflected local relational weaknesses, which undercut people's willingness to uphold the decision at the pastor's fellowship. Still, that should not have caused the members of the pastors' fellowship to have such a difficult time accepting the principle of upholding discipline. Indeed, discipline should be received as valid if it follows basic due process principles. It was wrong to make such a major issue of the lack of involvement of other local leaders. If we can reasonably give credence to a congregational court, in this case an ad hoc court, then we should!

Unfortunately, Assembly of God pastors accepted the principles as valid within their own denominations but could not see applying basic standards in a trans-denominational fellowship. That was a great lack. Should we eat with unrepentant adulterers or murderers at a pastors' fellowship? Shall we not ask those who judged the issue if repentance and restoration took place? The standards of discipline enjoin us to not eat with such a one. That is for all member of the Body. It is not limited to being applied as, "Do not eat with such a one in your denominational context."

Pastor Jacobs led a large charismatic congregation and on that basis was given credibility. He was a part of re-commissioning Pastor Wilkens. He and Pastor Wilkens claimed that due process was violated by the counsel of seven. Fellowship representatives could have at least investigated and questioned the counsel of seven to ascertain if due process was followed.

The size of Pastor Jacobs' congregation should not have influenced other pastors when he gave bad reports and did not follow due process himself. He needed to be corrected like anyone else. Searching questions on due process and real evidence should have been presented to expose his un-Scriptural action. Unfortunately, many members of the Body are still overly enamored by large size and external success. Of course, all of this advice would have been difficult to follow; the pastors would have had to been taught the principles of Scripture at the same time they were being asked to take Scriptural action.

Until pastors' fellowships accept the principles of discipline and covenant, they will continue to be either fellowships of unrighteousness or weak fellowships that are easy prey for the devil.

Illustration #3

This illustration shows us the devastating results of a congregation being structured so that the head leader is not accountable. It is true that the other leaders were stymied by the legal structure they had allowed. On the other hand, it was their responsibility to follow Matthew 18 and to seek to remove Pastor Simms. They should have approached the head leader as a plurality of leaders and demanded that he step down. All of the congregants should have been informed of the situation and called upon to follow the other elders. The building still might have been lost, but the congregation could have been saved. Perhaps even the building could have been saved.

The Scriptural commandments concerning discipline supersede any constitution or bylaws which contradict them. The bylaws of this congregation voided the commandments of God. The national association should have publicly exposed the situation and called upon the leader to give the assets to the ongoing congregation. Doing so could have informed the former congregants while encouraging them to follow the other elder leaders. Following these steps might not have worked, but this kind of pressure might have moved Pastor Simms.

Illustration #4

Because the Body today is so lacking in judicial process and righteous discipline, a case like this one is difficult to resolve. Yet it is important. It seems plain that the disfellowshipping congregations acted with due process and according to historic standards. The radio station and the host of the show that featured James Scott claimed that it was not their responsibility to deal with such issues; they were not a congregation. That is foolishness. As members of the Body, they are responsible for Scriptural norms. Therefore, to give the name "Christian" to a station and to allow leaders under discipline to use it as a platform is to undercut that discipline. The directors of the station were responsible as members of the Body to uphold the discipline of that congregation. It is that simple.

It is true that human charisma and continued ministry will enable one to eventually bypass discipline standards in today's Body in America. This is because the members and leaders are so lax. If a leader believes he was falsely disciplined, he should seek a court of appeal to hear all the evidence. It might lead to his exoneration or to the confirmation of the disciplining group. Even if there is disagreement between the two courts, at least it becomes clear to the Body that there is another reasonable perspective. Furthermore, any trained leader should recognize the difference between real repentance and the false repentance which says, "We are all sinners and God has forgiven me!" Yes, He has forgiven you – if you have *truly* repented. The idea of continuing in leadership under such circumstances is un-Scriptural notwithstanding the example of David. Read the account of what happened to David's family and to Israel after his sin. Is that what we want to invite upon the Body? The New Covenant calls for higher standards because we have the power of the Spirit so easily available to us.

Due to the lack of a consensus on standards and solid court structures, some are restored by God and truly repentant for the past without any clear decision having been rendered. In these cases, we may, until God has restored His Body more fully, have to rely on the fact that the confession and profession of repentance is truly a Scriptural one. "I was wrong; I had no excuse." There should be other leaders who can vouch for the stable and holy life now being lived. Furthermore, we should look for the leader to relate to elders in such a way that there is real accountability. Until the Body is restored to standards, some of the past may need to be overlooked to get on with the future. This future should find us maintaining Scriptural standards.

A leader disfellowshipped like the one in this case should at least make the grounds of his divorce clear – or his interpretation of the Scriptural standards on divorce and remarriage. Doing so would dispel confusion and allow people to decide to support his ministry or not, according to their own Scriptural convictions.

Illustration #5

How sad that men enter into covenants and yet so easily break them! A leader who is under discipline for serious sin and is given a righteous direction for restoration should not be trusted if he opts out of it. It is not only the sin of adultery or other gross sin. He is a covenant breaker. No one should receive the ministry of this person until he goes back and carries out the assigned discipline of restoration. If due process was followed, if a covenant bond of accountability was established and if the standards for restoration were basically reasonable for re-establishing standards of 1 Timothy 3, then all members of the Body should stand together against the brother continuing in ministry. The Body should not undercut discipline by supporting or endorsing such a leader.

If we would respond correctly, the person would be forced to take the proper spiritual medicine. In the process of counseling and sharing, the root causes of sin could be dealt with. In the context of covenant restoration, loneliness would be avoided and *true restoration* could take place. The denomination could have called upon the Body to support their discipline.

I realize there are cases where a man is in a denomination that does not believe in restoration. He may, in good conscience, be led to another credible group to provide this restoration. However, a quick reentry into ministry destroys both his and the group's credibility. Gross sin is evidence of major weaknesses that take time to be addressed. Establishing that 1 Timothy 3 is fulfilled takes a significant period of time.

One of the most abused Scriptures is the statement in Acts 5:29 (NAS) – *"We must obey God rather than men."* The context surrounding this verse is the authorities forbidding the disciples to obey the explicit command of Jesus to preach the gospel. How sad that many use this quote as grounds for disobeying elder authority in a process of accountability, restitution, and restoration! "The Spirit told me I am restored. I am accountable to God, not man. I must obey God rather than man." These statements misuse Scripture and are nothing but rubbish. Yet how often we have heard such Scriptures twisted in the mouths of the rebellious!

Illustration #6

In this case we have both a lack of Scriptural action by those who should hold the fallen leader accountable and a lack of right response by those who presumably know the inside story. This is a key point. We do not know that Rev. Howard Johnson really fell as was reported. How do we know there was no discipline? Indeed, ministers "in the know" are responsible for bringing their evidence to the leaders of the association and for holding the association accountable in applying Scriptural discipline. This discipline should include a public disclosure of the facts and the process of restoration that is to be followed.

If the association is in sin by failing to bring discipline, as in the case of Eli the priest, then a group of mature leaders who know the facts should, after having approached all levels of confrontation, officially disclose their evidence and the judgment they believe Scripture requires.

I do not believe that Scripture always requires us to cut ourselves off from the leaders who refuse to fully discipline – provided there is some discipline, however inadequate from our point of view. However, if there was no Scriptural discipline, how can we avoid the principle seen in the Hebrew Scriptures? A city that allows gross sin is itself to be punished by the other cities. I believe that allowing gross sin, for example unrepentant adultery or theft, without any repentance or a restoration process would require us to separate from the indulgent organization. For some, the fact that the sin is exposed and counseling and restitution ensues will be seen as adequate for maintaining fellowship with the group, even though the minister continues in ministry. This would at the least require some assurance of real accountability and of the fact that the minister is not continuing in sin. For others that would be too tolerant; they would break fellowship. I would maintain fellowship with people in the association, but certainly would not join or participate in the functions of an association that is so lax. I would urge stronger Scriptural standards for the association. However, if they continued to support one who fell into repeated sin, I do not see how anyone could Scripturally do anything but separate in such circumstances.

If the rumor is true, that the association did not discipline the fallen leader, then the association is in a place of serious sin. The association certainly should deal with this sin up front by public disclosure and the announcement of discipline. The rumor may be false, and if it is false, then sadly mistrust of the association and its leaders was spread.

Illustration #7

Two possibilities exist for this case. The leader being accused, Rev. David Spock, might or might not have fallen as the friend claimed. However, David Spock claims to have never fallen in this way. The denomination involved does not believe in restoration for fallen leaders. In addition, the denominational leaders profess to have made no decision concerning the leader that they will disclose.

When asked if there was a past disfellowshipping, the leaders say only that there is no present decision against the leader. They will not disclose any past sin.

It is possible that the denomination involved is remiss in its responsibilities. We may never know. However, since there is no documented evidence as part of a due process conclusion to prove that Pastor Spock fell, and since he professes that he did not so fall, the bad report is a rumor. It is sin to spread this report. Since his ministry bears good fruit and shows a solid family life, it would be wrong to separate from him on this basis. The same is true in the case of the friend's report against Jack Bixler. Without due process, nothing was shown – especially by rumors of twenty-five years ago.

Because the Body in America today does not discipline properly, we sometimes find ourselves in puzzling situations that are far below the ideal. Some ministers fell, truly repented, and over the years showed a righteous life. They did not have the benefit of Scriptural discipline and restoration. They were not connected to any structure of leaders that would properly restore. If their lives show years of stability, good fruit and a reflection of standards in 1 Timothy 3, I can accept that God did a work of restoration. God is the Restorer; human beings are the instruments. The fault belongs to the Body as a whole for the processes being such a mess. Some have been restored by God without due process because they genuinely sought God. Others who continue in ministry produce havoc because they opted out of Scriptural processes and standards.

Although we might accept ministers who truly repented while under a less than Scriptural process, that is no excuse for continuing to neglect Scriptural order in the Body today. Every minister should be connected to others intimately acquainted with him and who can vouch that standards of 1 Timothy 3 are being fulfilled. Acts 17:30 states – *"Truly, these times of ignorance God overlooked but now commands all men everywhere to repent."* The reader is no longer in ignorance now. God commands us to seek to uphold Scriptural standards and to join with those who will.

Illustration #8

Competition is a huge nemesis in the Body. Because of this spirit, we believe the worst of our brothers who are in leadership when disgruntled people whisper in our ears about them. Additionally, ministries compete for people by seeking to offer the best product, not so much to win the lost, but to affect the lateral transfer of members to their congregation. That is serious sin before the Lord. We seek to have the best show in town. It is amazing to note that, according to the advertising in a national Christian magazine, many large ministries each host the most important conference for everyone. Since many of them are scheduled for the same time, it is hard for the members of the Body to decide which of these most important conferences they need to attend. Conferences can be times of significant training and inspiration. However, conferences generally are not the most important events on the face of the earth today.

In the particular case here, the competing organization's leaders were only too glad to receive a bad report about the other organization and its leaders. They violated Scripture by receiving the brother without hearing the side of the slandered executives. This second group never checked out the divorce issues. The slandered executives might want to peruse the issue of the immorality of the other organization's receiving and spreading bad reports or slander. However, competition is so intense, it may not bring a cooperation that would affect reconciliation. At least the behavior of the sinning organization should be made known after due process.

Sadly, many people choose their involvements by the goose bumps raised and not by the integrity and justice of the organization. Oh that we would experience goose bumps when we see integrity, righteousness and justice! How can we bring justice to the nations when we are so full of injustice?

Illustration #9

Competition is again the root of the problem in this situation. The competition and kingdom-building continues because others in leadership allow it to continue. First, the leaders of the organization that is sinning should be confronted according to Matthew 18. If they are not willing to repent, other leaders and members of the Body should withdraw their support from the activities headed by the sinning leaders. Gross slander is serious.

In addition, many need to see that the Scriptural requirement is not to "refuse to take sides" or to "refuse to take up an offense." We have shown that attitude to be a false interpretation of Scripture. Rather Scripture, for love's sake, requires us to stand for justice. By feeding the monster of pride through support and cooperation with those in this sin, we never see the monster slain. Pride is slain when it does not gain its ends. The withdrawal of support would have a great effect, if not on the sinning leaders, at least for the Kingdom of God.

Scripture requires us to stand with those denied justice, with those who are abused and mistreated. It is especially applied to the poor who are so often exploited by the powerful. If we would so stand, the Body would see true love expressed in relationships and reflected in Scriptural norms of righteousness. The law of God is the expression of the love of God and of one's neighbor. Where His law is violated, love is surely absent.

Illustration #10

The error in this case is seeking to protect the fallen leader through privacy. As this case shows, covering up the sin of a fallen leader is contrary to Scripture and often backfires after the minister resumes ministry. The skeleton in the closet is somehow discovered and taken out for all to see. The right thing to do is to disclose the sin as well as the process of restoration that was undertaken, thereby clearing the air. Future unrighteous accusers are thwarted by the records and public knowledge of the truth, which is now part of the leader's resume and a testimony of God's grace to restore.

It is never too late to follow this process. As soon as this truth is understood, the leader should seek to document the facts from the past, as well as to gain the signatures of those who were involved in the discipline. He can than make the truth clearly known.

Illustration #11

The ability of leaders to believe the worst in this case was amazing to me. No one should have believed the evil reports being spread. Scriptural norms would have required us to ignore the reports unless Matthew 18 was followed. Following Scriptural injunctions would have led to a congregational court case to hear all of the evidence. Those who sit as elder judges in such a court need to take the time to hear all of the evidence as well as the rebuttal. Then a judgment should be rendered.

Accusers who refuse a fair court for decisions usually know that their case will not hold up under a more objective examination.

In this case, the accuser confused the people and other leaders by claiming that he followed Matthew 18. It is true that there were meetings of the first step. However, he never made it clear that he was unsatisfied with those meetings or that he was initiating the next steps in the process. At the third stage, a constituted and capable eldership needed to hear the whole case. Red flags should have flown in everyone's mind because there was no clear documentation or proof that those later steps outlined in Matthew 18 were accomplished or even properly attempted. The profession of following Matthew 18 by the accusing leader was a false profession.

I want to make it plain, however, that once Matthew 18 is violated and a severe dispute arises, it is no longer right to go back to the first steps of Matthew 18. It has become publicly known and is affecting many people. When this circumstance occurs, the applicable passage is 1 Corinthians 6. According to this chapter, we are to appoint judges to hear the issues and render a decision, with full evidence and testimony.

Men influenced by the evil one will seek to prolong a dispute indefinitely so that, by delaying tactics, evil might prevail. By word of mouth, the slander continues to be spread. One of the key norms of justice is that it be rendered swiftly.

Many leaders do not understand the norms of evidence and judgment. Judgment must not be subjective or intuitive. Some leaders do not want to take enough time to hear all of the evidence and to properly deliberate. They believe they do not have the time; their ministry responsibilities press upon them. The process could take several days, but important inter-congregational cases are well worth the time. The lack of such structure and judgment has taken far more time and energy from key leaders than a few days in court. Judges need to understand their role according to the principles in the Scripture as recounted in this book.

The situation we now speak of was investigated by Samuel Leslie. That was helpful, but inadequate. Those who made the accusations still needed to face the ones they accused before a fair court. Until then, the doubts concerning the accused and the accusing leader, Pastor Clements, will be widespread in the Body. Some of the air was cleared by the investigation, but not all of it.

We have a responsibility in love and justice to confront the accusing leader as well, that he might avoid a more serious judgment from God – especially if he is making false accusations. It seems that we find every way we can to avoid objective courts under qualified elders! Only a fair and sometimes in depth court within the Body can clear the air.

Conclusions

In these last days, God *will* have a people that fulfill the prayer of Jesus in John 17:21 – *"that they all may be one, as You, Father, are in Me, and I in You; that they also may be one in Us, that the world may believe that You sent Me."* This oneness will be achieved when we are filled with His Spirit, and from this filling we become intensely committed to His righteousness and His compassionate love. This oneness will be a product of God's full restoration of the equipping ministries in Ephesians 4:11ff, and as part of that an eldership according to Scriptural standards. The equipping ministries will train the people toward maturity. The eldership members of the equipping ministries will give themselves to enforcing God's standards of righteousness and ensuring the standards of 1 Timothy 3 for leaders. The eldership will assume their proper judicial role when required. That includes judging fairly in disputes, receiving and granting of transfers, issuing statements on divorce and remarriage, and disciplining – even to the point of disfellowshipping where necessary. This eldership will be a band of mutually accountable leaders who are motivated by the Good Shepherd's heart of love for the sheep.

As of 2015, American society is in a crisis. Heinous behavior is protected by law. Laws protecting the family and fostering traditional values have been jettisoned. We have failed to influence society toward righteousness and justice. The Reagan years were not a return to Scriptural norms. They were only a turn to traditional economic ideas, motivated by the financial setbacks of the Carter years. It was not a moral revival. The rate of teen promiscuity is at one of the highest levels in our history, despite AIDS and a host of other venereal diseases. Homosexual marriage is supported in many states, and at the time of this writing is winning in most of the state courts. The reason for this situation is not the evil of the secular humanists and the New Agers. It is, rather, the powerlessness of the Body in America. Because we have been a society that allows serious sin in its midst, we cannot turn our nation around. Only a just society, the congregation as a righteous counterculture, can affect our society in the right way. Only the concerted effort of multiple congregations in a locality can turn the tide.

We are called to be the salt and light of our society. Salt is a preservative and flavoring. What is the condition in America? The classical denominations have largely apostasized. The major exceptions are the Southern Baptists and Missouri Synod Lutherans. The American charismatic world is without clear standards and is tainted with scandals and non-accountability; the evangelical world is affected as well by this crisis of standards, but less than the charismatic world. We have allowed the world system to influence us. Evangelicals lack the power of God. The fundamentalist world is still largely isolated from engaging society and embracing their brothers in the Messiah because of a legalistic narrowness. A mighty revival is greatly needed to turn us to righteousness.

This revival has begun in movements in other nations, especially in the third world. Hundreds and even thousands of congregations that are moving in power and holiness are not famous in the media. We will see the Body in the twenty-first century arise when the religious empire of greed, competition, and injustice falls. It is Body of righteousness, justice, holiness and power in the Spirit; and it is burning with compassionate, God-inspired love.

APPENDIX 1

Letter of Transfer

Name of Congregation
Address of Congregation

The Board of Elders
Covenant Community Church
City, State, Zip

Dear Fellow Elders (or Pastor, whoever is to be addressed),

Mr. and Mrs. (or Mr., Mrs., Miss) are presently members in good standing of our congregation. We hereby transfer them to your oversight with our full recommendation.

Yours in His Service,
Name for the Board of Elders

_____

- -

Please mail this form when you receive (name) into membership so that we may be released from our responsibility.

Name of Congregation _____

Address of Congregation _____

We hereby do notify you that _____ has been received into the membership of our congregation.

Signature _____

Office/Position _____

APPENDIX II

Transfer When Not in Good Standing

Name of Congregation
Address of Congregation

The Board of Elders
Covenant Community Church
City, State, Zip

Dear Fellow Elders (or Pastor, whoever is to be addressed),

We hereby inform you that (Mr., Mrs., Miss,) _____is a member, but not in good standing in our congregation. The reason, according to our standards for membership, is (e.g. lack of attendance, financial support or service, or whatever other reasons would be related to the situation). We do not have any official or pending discipline with regard to gross sin or doctrinal error toward (him, her, them). We will therefore transfer (him, her, them) to your oversight with the recommendation that you seek to exhort (him, her, them) in these areas of concern.

Yours in His Service,

Name for the Board of Elders

- -

Please mail this form when you receive (name) into membership so that we may be released from our responsibility.

Name of Congregation _____
Address of Congregation _____

We hereby do notify you that _____ has been received into the membership of our congregation.

Signature _____

Office/Position _____

APPENDIX III

Refusal of Transfer

Name of Congregation
Address of Congregation

The Board of Elders
Covenant Community Church
City, State, Zip

Dear Fellow Elders (or Pastor, whoever is to be addressed),

We hereby inform you that we are unable to issue a transfer for (name or names). Our refusal is due to (enumerate gross sin or doctrinal error involved) _____.

We have carefully followed the process of Matthew 18 for loving confrontation and hereby enclose the records of our confrontation, testimony, evidence and our decision of (pending or completed) disfellowshipping. Please cooperate with us and work with the involved person(s) that (he, she, they) may be either reinstated to our membership or transferred to your charge. Please contact us so that we may work together in a redemptive way toward (his, her, their) restoration.

Yours in His Service,

Name for the Board of Elders

_____

Letter of Divorce

Name of Congregation
Address of Congregation

The Board of Elders
Covenant Community Church
City, State, Zip

To Whom It May Concern,

We, the Board of Elders, of (name of congregation) do hereby issue this letter of divorce to (full name of person). We believe they have the following Scriptural grounds for divorce with the right to remarry:

_____

_____

We have examined the evidence of this situation according to Scriptural standards of evidence and testimony. This letter grants the right to divorce and remarriage only upon obtaining the necessary right issued by the civil government for divorce and remarriage.

Sincerely,

Names

The Board of Elders

APPENDIX V

Membership Categories

The goal of recovering classical membership standards in a practical way has been fostered by our adopting the following categories in our membership rolls. We offer them to you for your consideration.

1) Provisional Members: those who are newly baptized or are newly transferred from another congregation. They have been given basic instruction before baptism concerning the fact that baptism is initiation into the community and a coming under eldership oversight. What this entails, with regard to discipline under the elders, if there is gross doctrinal sin or error, should be made clear. Such instruction can be done in a very brief time period (a half hour to an hour). Provisional members commit to seek full membership as part of their profession.

2) Full Membership in Good Standing: those who have completed the membership book either through the membership class or through home-group leader oversight and self-study. They are regularly attending, tithing and serving.

3) Membership Not in Good Standing: those provisional members who fail to fulfill full membership standards after a reasonable period of time or full members who fall for a period of time.

4) Under Discipline: those either disfellowshipped or presently in a process of discipline for gross doctrinal error or sin.

Those in categories one, two and three can be transferred and their status explained to the new pastor. Not all provisional members will remain where they were first received. Only those in category four should not be transferred.

APPENDIX VI

Provisional Membership

At Beth Messiah Congregation, we believed that a person who is immersed in the name of Yeshua under our auspices or who transfers to Beth Messiah should be immediately received into provisional membership. In New Testament times, immersion was understood as joining oneself to the local and corporate Body under the Lordship of the Messiah. This included coming under the authority or spiritual oversight of the elders of the community. Your acceptance of immersion or your transfer to Beth Messiah is a commitment of *provisional* membership which includes a commitment to seek full membership here or to transfer to another Bible-believing congregation, and commitment to accept the spiritual oversight of the elders of this community. This is similar to joining a nation and receiving citizenship. In this, one comes under the governing authority and the laws of that nation.

Eldership oversight at Beth Messiah included praying regularly for members, giving counsel, Scriptural teaching, training for spiritual service, correcting according to the Scripture, and disciplining for gross sin or doctrinal error if members fall away from the Lord. If one claims to be a follower of Yeshua while continuing in gross sin, one can be disfellowshipped. That means the members of Beth Messiah will be told that the person is to not be accepted as a member of the Body. We want all who either are immersed in water by us or who transfer their membership here to understand that civil courts in the United States have especially noted that congregations must make their standards clear to potential members before they have any right to enjoin Scriptural discipline.

We believe that eldership authority *does not* include requiring a member to order their personal life directions in accord with eldership counsel. Elders can only require that which Scripture clearly requires. Beyond basic membership standards, all members must be free to follow their conscience and the leading of the Holy Spirit for their personal life directions. We are committed to the importance of counsel and confirmation as part of congregational life, but we are also committed to safeguard our members against abuses of authority. One of these safeguards is our commitment to transfer any member, who is not under discipline for gross sin or error, to any Bible-believing congregation.

The step of immersion or transfer is a step of joining a special congregational family. What a privilege it is to serve one another together in the Kingdom of God!

APPENDIX VII

Gross Doctrinal Error

One of the great problems of the Body today is defining gross doctrinal error. This lack of definition has produced strife at levels beyond belief. Why? Leaders are willing to define gross doctrinal error as "whatever does not agree with my interpretations." Far too much is defined as essential and therefore becomes a basis for severe criticism of other ministers and groups. For example, we have seen extraordinary and slanderous criticism of other leaders and groups for the following reasons:

1) They believe in inner healing.
2) They believe in inner healing in the wrong way.
3) They do not believe in the *any moment pre-tribulation* return of the Lord.
4) They believe that the gospel we preach is the gospel of the Kingdom.
5) They believe that members of the Body can have a demon or be demonized (not possessed).
6) They do not believe in a literal millennial age wherein people would still be living in earthly bodies, marrying, and having children after Jesus returns (this view of no literal millennium is called amillennialism).
7) They believe in the integration of true insights in psychology with Christianity as helpful to counseling.

8) They believe the Holy Spirit teaches us, through life experience, things not *directly* in the Scriptures.
9) They believe that the latter rain movement was of God.
10) They believe that there are saved Roman Catholics.
11) They do not believe that prophets or those who exercise prophetic gifts must be 100 percent accurate.
12) They believe in dreams and visions from the Spirit.
13) They believe in positive confession of the Scripture to build faith.
14) They believe in the restoration of the function of apostles and prophets in the Body today (not in the sense of giving new doctrine).
15) They believe in a last days great harvest.
16) They believe in influencing society politically.

And so on, and so on. In my view, none of these issues are reasons for lambasting and discrediting other ministers or ministries. It is also a cardinal rule of fair criticism that we do not attack personally, and that *we represent the other's view to his satisfaction before criticizing. If we cannot do that, we have no right to criticize.* Dialogue in a good spirit through conversation and writing can aid in our finding truth; denunciations over these issues accomplish nothing. Furthermore, none of the listed issues involve gross doctrinal error sufficient for separating from other brothers and sisters.

Gross doctrinal error is defined by the classic creeds which are summarized in such statements as the one put forth by the National Association of Evangelicals. A group can define their official association more narrowly, but should not be engaged in denunciation of those who do not share the more narrrowly defined perspective.

We ourselves, at Beth Messiah and at Tikkun Ministries define our association of congregations with explicit statements that describe what we believe about Israel, Jewish calling, and the last days. Yet we fellowship with people who do not see all of our distinctive affirmations on these points.

We consider as brothers in fellowship those who embrace the classic doctrines of: the full inspiration and authority of the Scriptures (as the final and full authority of doctrine), the deity of Jesus, the triunity of God, the substitutionary atonement, resurrection and ascension of Jesus, His second coming, and final judgment. If they seek to test doctrine by the Scriptures, we can act as brothers even if we have differences on many issues.

Discipline for gross doctrinal error and public denunciation of wrong teaching should be limited to those areas considered classic doctrines. Other areas where we differ may be a reason for our going separate ways (different vision, approach and interpretation), but they should not be grounds for public denunciations, disfellowshippings, or other unrighteous modes of response.

Printed in the United States
By Bookmasters